FLIGHT OF THE TRAILER DOGS
LIFE IN AMERICA'S NEW MIDDLE CLASS

ELLEN GARRISON

NOMAD DOGS PUBLISHING

Flight of the Trailer Dogs

Life in America's New Middle Class

Written by Ellen Garrison

Nomad Dogs Publishing

LUKEWARM PRAISE FOR "FLIGHT"

I stink she may have cheat wiss my husband. She know too much stings. - Melanie Trump

I don't recaaaaw readin' that Trailer Dog book, but if'n urinall has proof to the contrary, then I reckon I musterd. - J. Sessions

I asked if I could be her spokesman. She told me to 'fuck off.' I hated the book. Or maybe not, if she changes her mind about that spokesman job. – Sean Spicer

Darn good book! – Sean Spicer

She's a feckless AND cunning linguist. – Samantha B.

Excellent book, perfect for a full-length movie with a proven box office draw in the lead. - Adam Sandler

I don't condone profanity and off-color humor in any form. It has ruined the moral fiber of our female youth and promoted drug use, along with pornographic imagery. – Bill Cosby

This crazy bitch again? Why she not drink tea I send her? - Vlad Putin

Not nearly enough profanity. This book sucks its own dick. – Tony the Mooch Scaramucci

Excellent reading, perfect for a full-length movie with a proven box office draw in the lead. – Kevin Spacey

WICH HUNT! – Trump

DEDICATION

"Trailer Dogs" everywhere.

You know who you are.

Geezers.

Kathy Griffin

If I ever DO make a Trailer Dogs movie

I would be honored if you played me

(Provided you're ok with wearing a fat suit)

RIP
Anthony Bourdain
You were a Trailer Dog at heart

PREFACE

After reading volumes 1 and 2, *Trailer Dogs* fans know that me and my old man sold our 29 foot 5th wheel at The Resort, and moved with our two dogs, Ben and Sully, to Oceanview RV Resort in the Pacific Northwest. Due to extreme laziness, my old man wanted to retire, and we were fed up living in a state redder than Trump's behind after it was spanked by Stormy Daniels.

We wanted to accomplish a number of things:

- Acquire a larger 5th wheel trailer than the one we'd been living in, one that wouldn't need repairs or a lot of maintenance

- Achieve serenity in a small town populated with sane, peace-loving people instead of gun-crazy, racist nut jobs disguised as Christians

- Enjoy the great outdoors more instead of being cooped up in a trailer in 120- degree temperatures

- Increase our savings doing things we enjoyed, like attending free wine-tasting events and redeeming coupons

- Purchase weed legally

Basically, we were trying to escape from the Idiocracy, and were seeking a pot of gold at the end of the rainbow. We were somewhat successful, in that we found the pot. Unfortunately, it didn't have any gold in it. We *did* achieve the last goal, however, as we no longer fear arrest and imprisonment. At least for buying the pot.

Flight of the Trailer Dogs is the story of our continuing struggles, told in my own inimitable style, and with the wickedly brilliant and sarcastic humor for which I am known, and in some circles, unduly reviled and oft-times unfairly censored. I'm looking at *you*, Twitter.

Readers will be pleased to learn that my old man will no longer be commenting or expressing his false criticisms in **Trailer Dogs**. As you well know from previous **TD** volumes, he fancied himself as my "manager" and demanded a high percentage of my earnings from the book in payment for computer-related editorial "services."

While he is a talented computer guy and a ***very special*** person in several respects, I have come to believe that I am fully capable of managing my own affairs without him dipping his paws into my personal honey bucket, if you catch my drift.

His firing ***was not***, as many might assume, due to the hundreds of emails I received calling me a "fucking moron," a "sociopathic twat," and a "fucking moron idiot foul-mouthed selfish cunt twat." To the contrary. I've not been able to prove it was he who was behind the vicious slurs, and in any case, as a strong advocate of strong free speech I would never deprive anyone of the right to express a negative opinion of me, providing it was a favorable one.

The truth is, I was going to fire my old man no matter if he had the goods on me or not, because WHEN I'M HIT, I HIT BACK TEN TIMES, SOMETIMES 573 TIMES HARDER.

Anyways, he agreed to continue performing computer tasks behind the scenes in exchange for being allowed to sleep indoors. I'll keep him around until I can find somebody else who'll work for free and who knows how to deliver a good foot massage.

I hope this clears up any confusion about my old man's firing. If not, readers may contact my Press Secretary, Mr. Sean Spicer, for additional information. Or, you can simply read my official tweets on a daily basis.

Writing a third, potentially Nobel Prize-winning memoir is not an easy task, as not anyone will tell you because they probably never wrote anything and should keep their damn mouths shut on the subject.

Trailer Dogs 3 almost didn't get written due to a lot of shit happening and the ridiculous amount of time I've been spending on

Twitter. Save for my perseverance and a dicey internet connection, you might not be about to enjoy the fascinating literary excursion ahead.

Thusly, as you navigate through stormy seas of profanity and uninhibited mockery of fucking-moron billionaire elites and memory-challenged geezers, don't forget this Fundamental Truth, one that will give you hope for the future of our beloved country and her beleaguered middle class: *NOTE TO SELF: Tell Spicer to stick something inspiring in here*

Bon voyage!

Ellen

AUTHOR'S NOTE: I regret to announce that Sean Spicer will be leaving his post as my Press Secretary, effective immediately. Sadly, Mr. Spicer is not as competent as he claimed to be, and he couldn't think of anything inspiring to stick in here. I wish the big idiot well.

WARNING

All of the characters in *Trailer Dogs 3*, whether or not they resemble living or dead people, are probably made up, because, as I keep trying to tell you people, how could they possibly be real?

Also, situations, names and places have been changed to protect me from lawsuits, which wouldn't do you any good, because I still don't have the kind of bread somebody like, say, Stephen King has for writing shit that isn't half as horrifying as my shit is. So, if you want to sue somebody, sue him.

EXCESSIVE PROFANITY WARNING

IN ADDITION TO OTHER REALLY OFFENSIVE LANGUAGE, THERE ARE APPROXIMATELY 78 INSTANCES OF THE WORD "FUCK" IN THIS BOOK. SO, IF YOU PLAN TO MAKE A BIG DEAL OUT OF IT AND GIVE IT A BAD REVIEW, *FUCK YOU*.

AUTHOR'S NOTE: OOPS, MAKE THAT 79.

TABLE OF CONTENTS

THIS PAGE LEFT INTENTIONALLY BLANK

BY STUPID STUPID STUPID MICROSOFT WORD

Regards,

Her Old Man

1 - THE ACQUISITION

Too Hot To Trot

As reported in *Trailer Dogs 2* (which you definitely need to purchase if only for the sex and implied violence), having had our fill of the sex and implied violence of the desert southwest, we bought a lot in an RV-oriented community called Oceanview, in the kinder and gentler Pacific Northwest where we'd lived years before.

After closing the deal on the lot, we returned to The Resort to sort out things and strategize what we hoped would be our final move before the Big Meat Wagon in the Sky swooped down with our tickets to ride.

Our lot when we first saw it

Back at The Resort, we became exhausted with all the strategizing and sorting out, so we decided to drive to Oceanview and spend the Christmas holidays there in our 23-foot travel trailer, which we'd left parked on the new lot.

Our plan went awry when we got back to the lot and found mushrooms the size of hubcaps growing along the bottom of the walls inside the trailer. The musty smell was so unpleasant, it would have put Roseanne off her chow for an hour, maybe an hour and a half.

Thoroughly demoralized, and with Christmas fast approaching, we checked into a motel and set out to find a trailer we could live in comfortably, and one that could accommodate a dehumidifier the size of Rhode Island.

Armed with Craigslist and local newspapers, we scoured areas within 30 miles of Oceanview. One trailer we looked at was an impressive 40′ feet long, but so horrific inside it could have been, and probably was, used as a Halloween spook house.

The orange-ish carpet had a large grayish oval that I took to be a stain, but soon realized was actually the *solitary clean spot* in a sea of dried cat piss.

Opening a cabinet under the galley sink, I noticed a small pile of shredded newspaper in one corner. When I saw the pile move ever so slightly, I slammed the cabinet door shut and nearly knocked my old man down getting the hell out of there.

Another trailer we found on Craigslist sounded like it had almost all the bells and whistles we were looking for, even though it was at the top of our price range.

We drove to the sellers' address in a relentless rainstorm, and while my old man braved the icy downpour checking the roof and exterior with a man named "Burt," I went inside with Maureen (call me 'Mo'), a harsh-looking battle ax if there ever was one.

Ensconced in the crook of Mo's left arm was a tiny Chihuahua, whose name Mo told me, was "Bitsy." I should say right here that I am a *huge* fan of Chihuahuas, no matter how fat and yappy they may be.

Mo explained that Bitsy was an "only dog," having lost his companion Chihuahua, Biddy, to a coyote that sneaked into their yard on the prowl for an afternoon snack. I no sooner got inside the trailer when Mo lit into her old man, Burt, as the person responsible for Biddy's untimely demise.

"Burt was always so jealous of Biddy," Mo sniffled. "She was my baby, and she got too much of my attention to suit him. So, he leaves her alone out in the yard one day, and pssst - a coyote comes up and drags her off."

Mo's eyes filled with tears. "I get home from the beauty salon and the son-of-a-bitch is there on that couch, eating popcorn and watching golf with Bitsy. All he says is 'a coyote ran off with your Biddy.' I looked everywhere for her and couldn't find a trace. I'll never forgive him for that. He's a horrible, horrible man."

Sensing that I might be intruding on a mental breakdown of sorts, or in the very least, the dissemination of too much fucking information, I tried to pick up the pace of my inspection of the trailer.

"Well, I guess I should take a quick look around so you can get back to what you were doing…"

"I never should have married that creep," Mo interjected.

"We met at the Elks about two months after my Charlie died, and there I was, a lonely, vulnerable widow. He took advantage of my grief. But don't get me wrong. The sex was unbelievable for a man his age. And he wasn't after my money - he has plenty of his own. Burt's kids from his first marriage are great, and he's wonderful to my two sons and their wives."

Momentarily left to my own devices, I started moving toward the kitchen area to check out the residential-size refrigerator. Mo, still toting Bitsy, was right behind me.

"Burt's not a dog person like I am," she continued. "He doesn't want them on the bed or furniture, and he won't allow me to feed them tidbits from the table. He barely tolerates poor little Bitsy who's still grieving over Biddy just like me."

I was beginning to sympathize with Mo and Bitsy about the treacherous Burt and his dog-hating, murderous ways. "How long has Biddy been gone?" I asked Mo, perfectly willing to testify in her behalf should Burt ever turn up with a shiv in his back.

"Over two years now," she whimpered. "But it's like it happened yesterday. I don't think Bitsy will ever be the same carefree little guy he used to be."

I had to admit, Bitsy **did** look kind of depressed. I reached over to comfort him with a friendly pat, and the little bastard sunk his teeth into my hand and wouldn't let go.

"Fucking christ!"

"See what I mean?" Mo said, less than apologetically. "Thanks to Burt, little Bitsy has trust issues."

Trust issues or not, approximately fifteen razor sharp needles were piercing my hand. After a while, apparently having satisfied his thirst for revenge or whatever the fuck he was feeling, Bitsy released me. Then he sat back on Mo's arm, glaring and snarling like an angry rat, and my sympathy for him started to dwindle some.

Mo, perhaps to divert attention from the tiny rows of puncture wounds and blood droplets forming on top of my hand, opened the big side-by-side refrigerator to demonstrate its capacity. The freezer side was chock full of meat.

"I don't suppose those steaks are included in the price..?" I half-joked, perhaps trying to rescue the situation from deteriorating any further than it already had. But Mo wasn't in the mood for humor.

"What's **that** supposed to mean? We're asking a lot less for this trailer than it's worth. You can check online and see for yourself."

Out of respect for the sanctity of life and a lengthy prison sentence, I ignored her and continued looking around. There was a stacked washer/dryer in a small closet, and a spacious living area with a nice looking sectional sofa. There was even a drop-down desk in a cabinet that would be a great place for me to write and post angry tweets throughout the day and night.

In the rear of the trailer was a bedroom, with a king-size bed and a huge clothes closet with shelves at the back for shoes and purses and snacks I could hide from my old man.

But the most desirable asset in the trailer, in my view, was there on the kitchen counter: a convection microwave.

I'd been lobbying for one of those babies for forever. It was a workhorse appliance that I could use to re-heat my coffee, warm up my sinus mask, AND pop my popcorn - all at the same time. Plus, my old man could easily learn to use it to thaw his TV dinners, or if he ever wanted to bake something for dessert.

I was fairly pissing myself with glee over these miraculous features as I walked to the front of the trailer, where I unexpectedly encountered a large swath of ripped-up flooring under a window.

Adjacent to it was a section of wall that had been cut away, exposing styrofoam-type insulation. The butchered wall had been partly hidden behind a lounge chair. Mo came over and stood beside me as I surveyed the destruction, which looked fairly substantial.

"We had a small leak there while we were away last year and Burt accidentally left the window open," she explained.

"You could throw a rug over that and no one would be the wiser." She paused then, and pursed her lips as if to chastise herself for not thinking to "throw a rug over it" *before* she started my tour.

Mo looked at me, narrowing her eyes. "We're not fixing it, if that's what you were thinking." I kept my mouth shut, not wanting her to know what I was thinking in case she had 911 on speed dial.

"What about the damage to the wall?" I ventured.

"Well, you could get a bigger chair to put in front of it, I guess" she said, with absolutely no sense of irony, or the danger she was putting herself in being so fucking snotty with me. "We're not going to fix that either, if that's what you're driving at."

I knew then and there we wouldn't be buying the trailer, but as I made my way to the door, I tried to let Mo down gently and with dignity, because of the lost Biddy, but mainly because that's just how I roll.

"Thanks for showing us your trailer." I said. "We'll go back to the motel and think about it, and I'll give you a call later on. And by the way, I sure do like that stacked washer & dryer set," I added, offering her a tiny ray of phony hope.

"You wouldn't if you had to wash anything bigger than a handkerchief," she responded. "It takes about three days to do a full load of clothes in that little piece of shit, and even longer to dry them. And you can forget about washing bed sheets altogether. I used it once and that was it."

I was still about three paces from the door, and my eyes darted around for something else I could compliment while executing my escape. *The convection microwave!*

"I've been wanting a convection microwave..."

"Well, you'll have to buy one for yourself, because I'm keeping this one and it's not included in the sale. And neither is the sectional couch. We already promised it to Burt's daughter, Marla."

I made it to the door just in time to nearly knock my old man backward down the steps. He was dripping wet, having been on the roof in the pouring rain, but he was smiling.

"Well, everything looks tight and solid on the roof," he said, "and the tires are fairly new. King Pin stabilizer is in good shape too, and -"

"That Stabilizer isn't included in the price," Burt cut in. "We're selling it separate from the trailer. You can make an offer on it if you want, though."

I grabbed my old man's arm and literally spun him around before he could say another word. He looked really dumb-struck and confused, but no more than usual.

"We've got a lot to think about, and thanks again for the tour, Mo" I said. "We'll give you a call when we've made up our minds."

"We go to bed at ten, so don't call here after that," Mo warned.

"Count on it, bitch-face," I muttered when we were well out of her hearing range. On the way back to the motel I filled my old man in on the ripped up floor and damaged wall.

"Mo claimed the damage was caused because Burt left a window open and rain blew in. But I know damn well that roof's leaking No question about it."

"I don't know about that…" my old man said. "The roof looks like it was re-sealed not that long ago, and the caulk was tight along the seams."

"Obviously, you didn't look close enough. The rain and lightning probably distracted you while you were on the roof," I said, rubbing dried blood spots off my hand.

"And in case you didn't notice, Mo is fucking nuts. You should have heard the mean, hateful things she said about Burt – her own husband! She even accused him of killing their dog, for goddsake!"

My old man shook his massive head, sending rivulets of rainwater down his gigantic nose and into the lines and crevasses in his wizened, time-ravaged face.

"Yep, they're a crazy-ass pair alright," he agreed. "Burt told me that Mo ran over their Chihuahua last year and then tried to blame it on a coyote… so who really knows? On the other hand, the trailer looks like it's in good condition."

I made no further comment, as I was super anxious to get back to the motel and try out some relaxation products we'd purchased that afternoon. My opinion wouldn't have mattered anyway, what with my old man being so gullible and such a know-it-all.

That evening around 7pm, the phone rang. Seeing that it was a call from Mo & Burt's number, my old man answered, and without saying a word, handed the phone to me.

"So, have you made up your mind on the trailer?" I heard Mo ask. "You were going to call back this evening and we haven't heard from you yet."

I didn't want to talk to Mo because of my intense hatred for her. Plus, I might have been using the aforementioned relaxation products, and it's never wise for me to have a conversation with an enemy when I'm feeling light-hearted and amiable. I took the only route available to me.

"Hoo dis calling?" I said in a high, sing-song voice.

"Dis - *this* is the people whose trailer you looked at today - Mo and Burt."

"No yogurt here, lady – you get wrong number!"

"This is the number *you* called *us* from to come and look at our trailer. You were just here earlier today!" Mo was clearly exasperated.

"This number not work good, lady. This number broke! We no fix!" And with that, I ended the call.

The Lyin' Truth

My old man laughed his ass off while I was on the phone with Mo, but despite a relaxation product-induced high, I was in no mood to join in the fun. Nothing was going right in our search for a trailer, and I was starting to think it might be a sign from the Universe telling us to go fuck ourselves.

Never one to give much of a shit what the Universe had to say, however, I went online and googled "oceanview used trailer." I was instantly rewarded with a link to an ad:

Used 36' 5th wheel trailer for sale. 3 Xlarge slide-outs, electric fireplace, garden tub-shower combo, 2 ACs, stacked washer/dryer, all in working order. $18,000

The ad included five pictures of the trailer, and it appeared to be in good shape inside and out. Even though we'd been hoping for a 40-footer, other features we saw in the pictures were right on the money. In fact, the money was right on the money, because we'd already decided that $18,500 was our upper limit.

What REALLY caught my attention in the ad, though, was the location of the trailer. It was literally parked 2 blocks from our lot at Oceanview. We'd driven by it multiple times since we got into town and hadn't noticed the "For Sale" sign. Now *this* was the kind of message from the Universe I could sink my teeth into.

The next morning we called the phone number in the ad and asked if we could drop by and look at the trailer ASAP.

The man who answered said he and his wife were preparing to meditate for an hour, but we were welcome to drop by any time after that. If the trailer turned out to be what we were looking for, we'd have to move fast, because they were going back to Nevada the day after Christmas.

They'd also put their Oceanview lot up for sale, and were mulling over an offer they'd just had on it. The prospective buyers had mentioned they might be interested in the 5th wheel as part of the deal, so we needed to take a look at the trailer before the buyers made up their minds about the trailer and before the sellers made up their minds about the lot offer.

After an hour had passed, we drove over in a cold drizzle to meet the sellers at their site. A very thin man with a gray beard and matching ponytail was standing on the covered patio next to a frizzy-haired woman wearing a long print skirt and a parka.

They reminded me a whole lot of the crazy-ass, born-again hippie couple who'd lived at The Resort in our old site next to Lonnie May.

I wasn't too keen on negotiating with another pair of Jesus freaks, but then again, I also wasn't too keen on setting up shop in a 23-foot travel trailer with two dogs and mushrooms sprouting out of the floor boards. The woman came up to me and extended both hands.

"I'm Truth, and this is my husband, Strength," she said, with a big smile, nodding toward the scrawny, pony-tailed man.

Holy shit, I thought to myself, what were two made-up names that would best describe me and my old man? I'm Wonder Woman Biggy-Titts, and this is my mate, His Lordship of Fartmonger? It was the only response I could think of, so I refrained from responding at all.

"Truth" ushered me inside the 5th wheel while Lord Fartmonger stayed outside with "Strength" to inspect the exterior and the roof. Once inside, I made up my mind that we were going to buy the trailer, taking into account its spaciousness and mushroom-free interior.

I was also attracted to an enticing aroma of pickles and olives in the air, the type of vegetables I'm most fond of. The smell, however, turned out to be plain vinegar, which Truth said she used exclusively as an environmentally responsible cleaning agent.

Truth offered me a seat in one of two recliners, and began to detail her background as a practitioner of Yoga and Mindfulness. She explained that she and Strength had purchased the Oceanview lot the year before, and had moved the trailer there from a park in Idaho.

A few months after that, while attending a Mindfulness convention in Nevada, they'd found an even more desirable property in a desert community where they could live among fellow Mindfulness disciples.

They'd bought a manufactured home, which was why they were anxious to sell the Oceanview lot *and* the trailer. They were looking forward to completing the transactions as expeditiously as possible so they could move on to Nevada, where, I supposed, they could meditate, ball each other's spouses on the sly, and do whatever the hell else hippy geezers did for shits and giggles these days.

Anyways, I was barely listening to Truth's spiel as I sat rocking in the *very* comfy recliner, taking in the roomy living area and enjoying warmth from the electric fireplace with its glowing fake embers and fake flames licking at the top of its fake firebox.

I was so comfortable, in fact, I almost forgot how much I wanted to get the hell out of this cold and rainy town and get back to the insufferable, debilitating heat of the desert southwest.

I could hear my old man clunking around on the roof above my head as Truth droned on and on about – whatever it was she was droning on and on about. But my ears pricked up when I heard her utter the words "full disclosure."

"In the interest of *full disclosure*, I need to tell you a few things about this trailer's past," she began in a hushed tone, as though she was about to reveal long-kept secrets of Opus Dei.

"Strength and I are the second owners. We bought the trailer from a couple we met in Idaho at a gathering of Yoga practitioners. They *seemed* like very nice people, even though they owned a cat and were meat-eaters."

I was immediately on the alert. "Were they Chinese by any chance?" I inquired. If we did end up buying the trailer, I didn't want to stumble upon any horrific "leftovers" in the cupboards or storage bins.

Truth seemed puzzled. "No, I believe they were from Dallas," she continued.

"Anyway, to make a long story short, they didn't tell us that the refrigerator had been acting up. About a month after we bought the trailer, the darn thing just conked out! We've been storing our vegetables and juices in a big cooler ever since. We didn't think it was karmically acceptable for them to have kept that information from us."

"How long have you owned the trailer again?" I asked.

"Going on three years now," Truth responded brightly. "It's been a great little home for us, but we've been spiritually called to move on."

On one hand, I was impressed with Truth's candor about the refrigerator troubles, but on the other hand I recalled that their ad had stated that *everything* was "in working order." Were there any other deficiencies Truth had omitted in her impatience to move to Nevada?

I was well aware of the dangers of impatience, and how being too hasty could impair a person's good judgment. At the same time, I was itching to get the hell out of Dodge – pronto - and to close a deal on a trailer as quickly as we possibly could.

"So, do you know what it would cost to replace the refrigerator?" I asked, demonstrating my well-honed negotiating skills.

"Strength called a local dealer, and they said it would be around $2,000 for a new fridge, including the labor to install it."

"Hmmm…then I suppose maybe the $18,000 you're asking for the trailer is a little too high, don't you agree? Wouldn't it be more karmically acceptable if the price was around $16,000 –that is, if someone were to offer that? Truth seemed to squirm a bit under my intense scrutiny.

"Well, Strength and I would have to talk it over, of course… We probably *should* come down that much, considering the fridge. But don't you want to see the rest of the trailer before you make an offer?"

"No need," I said, rising from the cozy comfort of the recliner, a bit worried that she'd change her mind before we got the cash in her hands. "We've seen the pictures. Everything looks tip top."

Strength and my old man came inside about then, both of them dripping wet after climbing all over the top of the trailer in a drizzle that had turned to steady rain. Truth dashed to the bathroom and brought them each a towel.

My old man dried off his drippy head and stood there looking kind of nervous. His eyes darted from me to the door as though he was trying to tell me something.

"Truth says she and Strength would consider a lower price on their trailer," I said. "So I offered $16,000 instead of $18,000 on account of the refrigerator needs to be replaced. Truth told me that would probably be ok with Strength. That's a good deal for both parties, don't you think?"

Strength was nodding enthusiastically, but my old man's eyes were moving back and forth faster and faster, and I thought for a minute he was having some kind of seizure. Finally, they remained steady and fixed on me.

"I think maybe we should go back to the motel room and talk about it, don't you, *dear*?" he said, annunciating each word as though he was dealing with a 3-year old who couldn't comprehend shit. I brushed aside his condescending attitude and proceeded with negotiations. I knew that I alone could do it.

That morning we wrote a check to Truth and Strength, whose real names were Debby and Gary Barnes. For $16,000, we had purchased:

A pickle-smelling trailer with a busted refrigerator, a non-working oven, a broken range fan, a toilet that wouldn't hold water, a malfunctioning stacked washer/dryer that at some point had leaked all over its alcove and soaked into the wood underlayment, carpeting (hidden under a large area rug), that was so damp and filthy from the leaky roof, Ben and Sully refused to skootch their butts across it.

And oh, I almost forgot: an awning that was rotten and in tatters when it unfurled, and an electric fireplace that stopped working the second time we turned it on.

THE MORAL OF THIS STORY

Haste and impatience are almost *always* the cause of terrible decisions, - decisions that can lead to my old man catching hell for the next 6-12 months. For you see, in his haste and impatience to report on leaky areas he'd noticed while on the roof of Truth and Strength's trailer, he made a terribly rash decision: He called me "dear."

After all these years, he should have known better.

2 - THE FINAL DAYS

Shortly after we closed the deal on the rolling Titanic, we hired a local guy ($100) to tow it to an RV shop where they replaced the refrigerator ($2500-fridge and labor). Then we hired the guy again ($100) to tow it to back Oceanview.

By that time it was two days before Christmas and we needed to get back to The Resort to take care of some things and say our final goodbyes.

Out of an abundance of caution (and fear of more mushrooms sprouting from the floor), we bought two large dehumidifiers, stationing one in the smaller travel trailer and one in the big trailer. We left the power on and arranged hoses from the dehumidifiers to the trailers' shower compartments to drain.

After covering the roofs of both trailers with tarps, we locked everything, jumped in the Prius, and headed south. The traffic was surprisingly light for the holidays, and it felt good to be out of the rain.

Once back at The Resort, we began to take stock of items we wanted to keep and things we might be able to sell. My old man, who'd been all set to retire permanently from the rat race, was asked by his employer if he'd stay on for another 3-6 months, working part time as a consultant. He agreed, providing he could work remotely from Oceanview.

By the end of January, we had a fairly decent plan for our escape that included renting a large U-Haul trailer for things we just couldn't bear to part with, or needed to set up housekeeping at Oceanview.

Some of our pals at The Resort who were living there permanently, and others who were seasonal snowbirds, would probably be interested in buying our "leftovers" if the price was right. Anything that didn't sell would be donated to the thrift shop.

February came and went, and by mid-March it was already getting so uncomfortably hot that quite a few of the snowbirds, including Phyllis and Bill Crane, decided to pack up early and go back to their northern homes.

The uncommonly hot weather continued into April, and that had many climate change deniers wondering if perhaps they had been fooled by scientific mumbo-jumbo into thinking global warming was a hoax. In any case, we decided to move up our departure date to early May.

Virginia Lopp, my geezer buddy and new co-owner of The Resort with Gerald Karn, took off to visit her sister in California. Although her daughters were still around, Claudia had taken a part-time job at the Sheriff's office, and Laurette Lopp was managing The Resort's office.

Laurette's boyfriend, Gerald Karn, previously noted co-owner of The Resort, was busy doing repairs around the park. We didn't see much of them during that period, even though Gerald had bought our 5th wheel and had insisted on paying cash for it before we even moved out.

Two year-round residents – Lonnie May and Cripple Jon – we still saw on a daily basis, because they lurked around our site like a pair of vultures, waiting for the first whiff of decaying meat. The scavengers probably figured we might set out something valuable next to the dumpster, and they could re-sell it at the local weekend swap meet.

Other Resort residents had moved out completely and weren't coming back. Church Lady, transgender according to park gossip, left when The Resort's new management announced plans to install a shooting range instead of a chapel in the space formerly occupied by the ruined Cornhole Court.

"Church Lady," as I'd nicknamed her (because every time I saw her she was smoking and reading the Bible in her lawn chair) had lobbied long and hard to become head Pastor or Pastress (whatever the case may be) at the proposed house of worship.

Being the solid Christians they were, however, park residents would have none of that, and they not only nixed the chapel idea, but voted to excommunicate Church Lady for his/her sinful ways and his/her disregard for the Second Amendment. Sadly, my friend Virginia Lopp spearheaded the excommunication.

After consulting local regulations and building codes, however, the new management had to scrap plans for its wildly popular and highly anticipated shooting range. Immediately thereafter, Dottie Ballou put her 5th wheel trailer up for sale and moved to an apartment.

"I ain't livin' nowhere where guns ain't welcome," Dottie confided to me as she taped an orange FOR SALE sign to the front of her trailer. "My new apartment is right up the road, and I can bear my arms and walk over to the gun club any goddamn time I want."

Ten days before we were scheduled to leave for Oceanview, and as always seemed to happen to us, the 5th wheel's water heater went on the fritz and my old man had to order a replacement.

Although we doubted that Gerald Karn would care one way or another (since he was spending most of his time shacked up at Laurette Lopp's trailer), neither of us relished taking cold showers for the rest of our stay despite the miserably hot weather. At night it can get pretty damn cold in the middle of nowhere.

The new water heater was delivered a couple days later, just about the same time the rig's house battery conked out. The hydraulic slide-out mechanisms and the hitch wouldn't work without it, so we had to buy a new battery and swap it out.

I felt like we'd skipped over Limbo and were stuck at The Resort forever. My Mom's prophecy had come to pass: *I was roasting in Hell for all eternity.*

Then Ben, our elderly Yorki-Poo, had a weird incident, and nothing else mattered at all to us, not even roasting in Hell.

Ben's "spell" happened while I was packing up extra dishes and my old man was at his office, finishing some last minute reports. Closing in on 18 years, Ben had been showing more and more sensitivity to warm weather, to the point he didn't want to go outside - for any reason, least of all to poop or pee.

The minute I'd get him outside the trailer, he'd sit down and refuse to budge. I started taking the boys out separately, picking Ben up and carrying him to his nearby pooping grounds, then carrying him back inside again. He spent most of the day snoozing on the couch in front of the tiny window air conditioner, rising only to wolf down his food and bark at imaginary enemies.

I had just wrapped a dinner plate in newspaper when a loud yowl nearly caused me to soil myself. Ben had been napping peacefully under the AC, when suddenly he sprang up, leapt from the couch, and started running back and forth through the trailer.

Turds were flying out of his butt like corn from a popper, and he was wild-eyed and barking. Sully joined in the melee, and both of them were out of control. I finally managed to grab Ben and hold onto him.

The old boy was panicked and making ungodly sounds, and I thought he might be having a heart attack or stroke. I quieted him down a little, grabbed a bottle of baby aspirin and speed-dialed my old man at work.

While I rolled an aspirin into cream cheese and fed it to Ben (in case he *was* having a heart attack), I filled him in on what was going on.

"He probably just had to poop," my old man pointed out. "You know how crotchety he gets when he needs to poop and can't get our attention."

"This was different. You should have heard the noises he was making." At that very moment Ben went rigid in my lap and started to howl again.

"I'll be right there," my old man said, abruptly ending the call.

Meanwhile, under the dining table, poor Sully was crouched and shaking like a leaf. I wrapped Ben in a towel and held him close again. Sully jumped up beside us, watching Ben intently and glancing at me as if to ask why I wasn't making this nightmare stop.

By the time my old man got back to The Resort (he made the 45 minute trip in under 30 minutes), Ben had recovered completely and was resting comfortably on the couch under the AC as though nothing had happened.

When my old man walked through the door, he jumped down and started leaping around in circles of happiness as he always did when one or the other of us came home.

"See what I told you," my old man said with a nervous laugh. "The old guy just had to poop and you weren't paying attention to his signals."

I wasn't so sure about that, and I didn't think he was either. But one thing *did* seem sure. Ben would live to crap on the floor another day.

Black Saturday

Replacing the water heater really ate into time we needed to do other things, like dismantling two plastic sheds, unloading their contents, and packing up everything we could fit into a 12' X 8' UHaul trailer, our pickup truck, and the car.

Despite the fact that we had down-sized several times in the past three years, we still had more shit than Chris Christie's outhouse, some of it gathering dust in a rented storage unit near town. We had to get rid of it fast.

On Friday, a week before we were scheduled to leave, I called Dottie Ballou and asked if she was interested in any of our stuff to furnish her new apartment. She said she was basically sleeping on the floor, had no rugs, no living room or bedroom furniture, not even a picture to hang on the wall.

The one item Dottie had bought for her new crib was a gun rack, and it was her only furniture thus far. I arranged to meet her at our storage unit, and after briefly looking over the merchandise, she bought almost everything we had - on the spot, with no quibbling over the prices.

I helped her load end tables, chairs, rugs, paintings, large flat screen TV, etc., onto her truck and our truck, and we schlepped them back to her place.

Her apartment was pretty nice. The units were 4 to a complex, and the architecture was adobe style. Dottie's unit was on the ground floor, had two decent-size bedrooms and two bathrooms, one with a nice big tub-shower combo.

A kiva fireplace was in one corner of the living room, and beyond sliding glass doors was a covered patio that had an attached utility closet with a water heater and hook ups for a washer and dryer. A small fenced garden beyond the patio was perfect for Dottie's two dogs, who, based on fecal evidence, had already claimed it for themselves.

The place was crowded with moving boxes, which were overflowing with blankets, clothing, and back issues of *Guns & Ammo*. A wobbly kitchen table, left behind by previous tenants, held a mother lode of booze, mostly whiskey.

After we unloaded her purchases, Dottie paid me in cash and invited me to have a celebratory drink with her. Remembering her proclivity for drunken target practice, I declined, promising to come back after she'd arranged her new furniture and put away all the crap she had laying around. Before I left, she pulled another $50 out of her billfold, having decided to buy the small chest freezer still at our storage unit.

"I'm gonna do a lot of huntin' next fall, and I need somewhere to put meat. That is, if fuckin' Trump don't come for my guns," she said with a shrug. I was a little taken aback.

"Dottie, if Obama didn't come for your guns, what makes you think Trump will?" She pondered the question a bit.

"I ain't sure…there's just *something* about that son of a bitch I don't trust. But if he can get the Mexes to pay for his wall, that's good enough for me."

I left Dottie to her delusions and her unpacking, and headed back to The Resort. Noting what we had left to get rid of, I called a few year-rounders to let them know I was going to offer fabulous merchandise at rock-bottom prices.

Ten minutes later, just about everyone still residing at the park showed up asking to see the goods. I told them to come back the next day - Saturday - when it would all be on display.

At a quarter to six the next morning, we were awakened by someone pounding on the door. I threw on my robe and peered out the galley window. It was Lonnie May, standing there in his usual grimy uniform that looked like something he'd borrowed from a zombie.

"I heard through the grape line you was sellin' some stuff. So where is it?" he demanded, pausing to hock up a wad of nastiness toward the street.

I momentarily pictured myself reaching for a butcher knife and flinging myself at him ala Norman Bates, but the knife was in a drawer, and my reflexes weren't what they used to be. Plus, I would have to kill Daisy May (leave no witnesses), and despite my homicidal feelings toward Lonnie, I couldn't bring myself to do away with his dog.

"Come back around 10. I'll have it all set up by then." Lonnie looked at me as though he couldn't believe his ears.

"Ten o'clock? Hell, woman, don't you think I got better things to do than wait around here 'til tenfuckino'clock?"

I opened my mouth, then shut it. It never did any good to try to reason with Lonnie or even get sarcastic with him. He was a solid brick of humorless self-interest. I took a deep breath and put on my best cloak of civility.

"Well, then come back at nine, and if I don't have everything set up and ready to go by then, you can kiss my fucking ass. How about *that*?"

To my surprise, he nodded. The asshat thought he'd *won a concession* from me! I pulled the door shut and shuffled back to bed. My old man and the dogs were still snoozing. I sprawled there, exhausted and fuming. Unable to fall back to sleep, I got up and started a pot of coffee.

I had a rubbery taste in my mouth, and something was scraping the inside of my left cheek. I stuck a finger in and fished out part of the plastic tooth guard that prevented me from grinding my teeth into chalk while I slept. I had chewed the damn thing in half. I tried not to think where the other half was.

At 8:00am my old man left in the truck to run some errands in town, and I went outside to start organizing things for the sale. I put two folding tables end to end, set sale items on top and began pricing them.

I'd only got a few prices on when folks walked up and started milling around the tables, asking what this and that cost before I'd had the chance to tag it. I told them to come back in half an hour and everything would be ready. Instead, they congregated out in the street, where they stood waiting expectantly like Walmart shoppers on Thanksgiving night.

Finally, when I had tagged the last item, I signaled the crowd that the sale could begin, and they all surged forward. Lonnie May was at the forefront, and Cripple Jon, proudly wearing a red MAGA cap, was behind him in his wheel chair.

Several of the browsers, wary of a possible sting operation when they saw how cheap everything was, asked if they had read the price correctly. Then they pulled a couple bucks out of their pockets, grabbed the loot, and scurried off. Everybody, of course, except Lonnie May.

With Daisy May snuffling around at his side, Lonnie picked up various articles and examined them with great care (something he should have done years ago when he chopped off two of his own fingers while using a table saw). I watched him frown as he inspected the cover of a DVD.

Lonnie removed the disc from its case and held it up to the light with the two remaining fingers of his hand. He was obviously looking for a blemish or small defect that might bring the price down from 50 cents to a quarter.

Finding nothing to haggle over, he returned the disc to its case and picked up a toaster, subjecting it to equally meticulous review. His eyes narrowed and he looked up at me like he'd just found the smoking gun in one of Hillary's 30,000 emails.

I'd priced the toaster at two dollars. It wasn't an expensive model, but it was new. I'd bought it to use in our 23-foot trailer, then realized we could use the toaster we already had.

At 15 bucks it hadn't been worth the cost of gas for the 40-mile round trip to take it back for a refund. Lonnie turned the toaster sideways and peered into its two bread slots like he was checking under the hood of a Mazerati.

"This thing work?"

"It should, Lonnie. It's brand new."

"There's fingerprints on it, like maybe somebody already bought it before you and then brung it back 'cause it didn't work, and then they just went and put it back on the shelf."

Noting Lonnie's grubby hands, I was pretty sure the fingerprints came from his own greasy paws. He wasn't through criticizing the quality of the merchandise.

"When I turned it kitty wampus," he went on, "some crumbs fell out."

"Well, I guess that proves it works, doesn't it, Lonnie?"

"Don't know about that," he grunted, unsatisfied with my observation. At that moment, two female shoppers walked up to browse. One of them stood next to Lonnie, eyeing the toaster.

"You buying that toaster?" she asked. "Because if you don't want it, I do."

Lonnie cast a sneer her way. "I ain't made up my mind yet, lady."

Still clutching the toaster, Lonnie proceeded to walk over to the two practically new "gravity" loungers I was offering for $10 each.

"Is that 10 bucks each or $10 for the both of 'em?"

Before I could answer, the companion of the women who wanted the toaster spoke up. "I'm buying both of those chairs," she announced, pulling a twenty dollar bill out of her pocket. She folded up the chairs, hung one off each arm, and waltzed past Lonnie. His face turned bright red. He was livid.

"Here's 2 bucks for the fuckin' toaster, but if it don't work, I'm gonna expect a refund."

Behind him, the woman who'd been waiting for his decision on the toaster, shook her head and muttered "shithead" under her breath. More park residents had gathered to browse the sale area, and space was getting a little tight.

Navigating the crowd, Cripple Jon ran his wheelchair over Lonnie's left foot. Lonnie let out a yelp, and Daisy May came dashing over to see if there was any biting to be done. Lonnie bent down and scratched her ear with a free hand.

"It's ok, girlie" he comforted her. "That son of bitch never looks where he's goin' except when he's suckin' up to them Lopps."

Virginia Lopp and her daughters, Claudia and Laurette, were the new co-owners of The Resort, along with Laurette's beau, Gerald Karn. Gerald Karn was Lonnie May's long-time rival and sworn enemy. It might not have been the case had Gerald not won a bundle on a lottery scratch ticket a couple years earlier.

Since then, overcome with jealousy, Lonnie hadn't missed a chance to paint Gerald as a loser. Mightily offended by the implication that he was a suck up, Cripple Jon swung his chair around.

"You thut your goddamn mouth, Lonnie. You and your mutt can kith my ath."

Lonnie snorted, and Daisy May lowered her head in obvious disgust. I was feeling a familiar hatred for Lonnie *and* for Cripple Jon begin to simmer in my psyche pot. Several of my would-be customers, fearing a brouhaha was about to develop, started to back away. It seemed like a good time for an intervention.

"Look here," I said in my best Walmart manager's voice, "I have other shit I need to do today, so I'll tell you what. This sale is going to end in 15 minutes. Then I'll take what's left down to Rosie's Thrift Shop and donate it."

I knew the effect my announcement would have on the bargain hunters. Prices at Rosie's Thrift Shop would be a lot higher than mine, and none of them wanted that.

All at once they rushed back over and started scooping up anything they could carry. Pretty soon I had a hand full of greenbacks and the showroom was all but empty.

"How much for the al up there on the roof?" Lonnie May demanded, pointing to the large plastic *owl* we'd put on top of the 5th wheel to discourage pigeons from crapping on the rig, car and truck.

I hadn't even thought about the owl. In fact, it didn't work as advertised. Not only did pigeons and mourning doves still shit all over our vehicles and windows, they targeted the owl in particular, and its weirdly bobbing head and plastic shoulders were covered in bird shit. If Lonnie hadn't asked about it, I would have tossed it in the dumpster.

"You can have it for 5 bucks," I told him. "But you'll have to wait 'til my old man gets home so he can get it down with the ladder. It's full of rocks and it's **really** heavy."

Cripple Jon spoke up. "I'll give you $10 for that al. I need that al worth than Lonnie. Them damn birdths thit all over my park model and ith hard for me to reach the mop up there."

Sensing he might lose yet another incredible bargain, Lonnie set his toaster on the concrete pad next to our rig.

"Forget it, Jonny. I already sealed the deal on that al," he muttered, handing me a five dollar bill and smirking at Cripple Jon. "I'm goin' over to my trailer and get a pole and get that al down right here and now."

With that, he swaggered off across the street and went into his storage shed. He was back in a minute with a skinny 6-foot pipe, which he began using to poke at the al.

"Don't, Lonnie," I shouted, but not before he'd tipped the owl forward, causing it to tumble and roll beak-first off the top of the trailer. We all watched as it hit the ground and shattered, scattering its belly full of rocks on the concrete slab.

Only the owl's shit-covered head had survived intact, and it sat there, bobbing dejectedly alongside jagged fragments of its plastic, shit-covered body. Lonnie May, mouth agape, was stunned. Even Daisy May seemed to be in a state of shock, uncertain of who was responsible for the catastrophe.

Cripple Jon leaned sideways in his wheelchair and started laughing. Several spectators, standing well out of harm's way, joined in. I suppressed a guffaw of my own as I waited to hear what brilliant observation Lonnie was going to make about the disaster, and whom he was going to blame for it. I was soon rewarded.

"That al was deflective. It wasn't truthful advertisin' sellin' it when it was already cracked up."

"You broke it, you bought it, ath hole," Cripple Jon snorted, and the onlookers nodded and murmured their endorsement.

"I ain't payin' for no broke shit, you whiny, little ass-kissin' maggot!" Lonnie May broke in.

"You done paid for it, dumb ath," CJ responded, "And don't be callin' me no maggot. You was for Trump all the way before you found out he might take away your goverment handouths."

"Them ain't handouts!" Lonnie May shouted. "I paid for them handouts out of my withheld taxes. And you got some brass since you been dippin' in handouts for years and never even had no decent job!"

For a minute I thought Lonnie might strike Cripple Jon, but instead, he reached out and snatched the MAGA cap off Jon's head and tossed it toward the street like a frisbee.

Daisy May, ever alert and ever off-leash, loped away, scooping up the hat and retreating to the steps of Lonnie's trailer. And there she sat, MAGA cap in her jaws, daring anyone to try and make America great again.

"Well, well, well," Lonnie gloated. "Looks like the little maggot hat's on the other foot now, ain't it Jonny?"

At that moment, my old man drove up unexpectedly. Unfortunately, he didn't notice the toaster Lonnie had left sitting on the concrete pad while he was fetching the al pipe. The sound of a big truck tire crushing stainless steel and plastic momentarily silenced us all. My old man, looking none too happy, hopped out and peered under the truck.

"What the hell was that?" he wanted to know.

"Ith Lonnie Mayth toathster," Cripple Jon solemnly informed him.

I peeled seven bucks off the top of my wad of bills and walked over to Lonnie May. "Here's for the owl and the toaster. Now get out of here before I shove that pipe up your ass sideways."

Cripple Jon started to laugh again, but stifled it when he saw the look in my eye and realized his own ass was in mortal danger.

The crowd dispersed quickly then, Lonnie May slouching resentfully across the street toward his trailer, with Cripple Jon rolling along behind him, probably hoping to negotiate a settlement with Daisy May over his confiscated MAGA hat.

My old man opened the door to our trailer and we went inside, not speaking. The boys started carrying on and jumping around until Sully knocked over their bowl and sent water flying every which way.

I grabbed a fistful of paper towels, got down on my hands and knees and began to sop it up. While I was down there on the floor, I noticed two small turds lurking under the table.

Hard to tell how long they'd been there, but from experience, and based on their shape and size, I knew they were Ben's. I stood up to get more paper towels and banged my head on the corner of the table.

Three more days and we'd be out of here... I sighed in delicious anticipation. The goose egg forming on the side of my head barely hurt at all.

THE MORAL OF THIS STORY

When you're cleaning dog shit from under a table in a trailer, don't stand up fast.

3 - INTERIOR DESIGN, BY DOTTIE BALLOU

The Monday after I helped Dottie Ballou haul the things she'd bought from us to her new apartment, she called and asked if she could drop by and pick up the small chest freezer left at our storage unit.

It was the last item there, and we needed to sweep the unit and close the account. I met her in the morning, and we hoisted the freezer into the bed of her truck and drove back to her apartment. She was super excited to show me how she'd incorporated our furniture, rugs and art into her décor.

"You're gonna flip your wig, girl," she told me enthusiastically. "It's a real showplace now."

When we arrived at the graveled parking area in front of the apartment, I was a little surprised to see that Dottie had bought a menagerie of resin yard animals and gnomes and whirling whirligigs on sticks, and had placed them side-by-side in neat rows in the un-landscaped dirt next to the entry door.

The outdoor tableau was somewhat reminiscent of Laurette Lopp's trailer site decorations without the whimsy and carelessly artful charm of Laurette's gnomes and fairies.

If anything, Dottie's plastic army more resembled a regimental formation of Hitler youth, celebrating the Fuhrer's birthday at Chuck E. Cheese. It was appalling. Noticing my speechless wonderment, Dottie beamed.

"You ain't seen nothin' yet," she said. "Wait till you see the statue I got for the patio."

We went inside, and I caught my breath at the sight of what Dottie had accomplished in the space of a several days: *Absolutely nothing.* The boxes of clothes were still there, pants, shirts and underwear spilling over the sides.

The only difference I could detect was that Dottie had set some of the boxes *on top* of furniture she'd bought from us. A few of our paintings were hung so high on the walls I had to crane my neck to view them.

I almost wept when I saw that she'd replaced the shades on our rather expensive southwestern table lamps with frilly, under-sized shades that still had plastic wrappers on them.

She led me into the bedroom where we were greeted by a king-size mattress on the floor next to an as-of-yet uncrated bed. The mattress was covered with a sleeping bag upon which Dottie's two dogs were grooming their nether regions on more cast-off articles of her clothing.

An empty bottle of Jim Beam was on the floor next to the bed, and Dottie, uncharacteristically embarrassed, snatched up the empty and tossed it onto a pile of clothes protruding from yet another unpacked box.

"Your chester drawers is gonna work out real good, once I get the time to put my own drawers in it," she noted, chuckling at her little joke.

I glanced through the open bathroom door and saw that nothing had been done in there either, save for the addition of a night light on a stand on top of the vanity. It was a purple, three-dimensional torso of Jesus, hanging pitifully on the cross. The somewhat out-of-place modern relic parted a wide sea of deodorants, mouthwash, hairbrushes, and still-damp towels.

We walked back to the kitchen, which appeared to be the only room in the apartment that Dottie had actually organized -with her collection of booze, which topped the refrigerator and spilled over onto the counter next to the sink.

On the round dining table were 4 placemats, each with a different brightly-colored cartoonish owl face. A ceramic vase, which was the head of a lime-green owl with yellow eyes and a blue bow tie, served as a centerpiece. I was at a loss for words. Dottie took my dumb-founded silence as further acknowledgement of her decorating talent.

"I *know*," she said with a sly grin. "Ain't they just the cutest goddamn things you ever saw?"

Now she was ready to show me her pièce de résistance on the patio. She theatrically pulled back the curtain and slid the glass door open.

There, just beyond the edge of the concrete slab, was a resin statue of a naked, morbidly obese man, with flabby man-boobs and a fig leaf covering his genital area. Had it not been for the full head of carved wavy hair and absence of a MAGA cap, I would have sworn it was Trump himself.

"It's a replica of the statue in all the big museums," Dottie informed me. "That Michael Angelo must have been awful well-hung, considerin' the size of the leaf on his pecker."

She broke into gales of laughter, which led to a coughing fit, which led to a loud, trumpeting fart, which led to me having to race back inside to the bathroom. I made it barely in the nick of time.

I had neither the bladder capacity, nor the spare underwear to explain to Dottie that the statue was a plastic *caricature* of "David," Michelangelo's world famous sculpture, and I doubted that she would have believed me anyway.

I congratulated Dottie on her fantastic interior decoration skills, hugged her goodbye, and made my way to the front door, pausing to write down the website where she'd ordered the plastic statue. It was kind of expensive at $125 plus shipping, but that didn't bother me at all. It was *exactly* the type of thing I had envisioned for our yard at Oceanview.

THE MORAL OF THIS STORY

When it comes to acquiring priceless classical art that will give years of happiness and viewing satisfaction, its cost should never be a deciding factor. Unless, of course, it interferes with your ability to afford a good supply of weed and/or box wine. In that case, *fuck* the art.

4 - LONNIE MAY'S LAST STAND

The morning of our departure from The Resort dawned hot, dry and windy. My old man left to pick up the UHaul trailer he'd rented, while I stayed behind to defrost the refrigerator, pack up last minute bedding and toiletries, and prepare Sully and Ben for the long trip ahead.

Ben would be riding shotgun in the truck with my old man, and Sully was traveling with me in the Prius.

I'd bought the boys each a bed pillow to sit on and seat belt attachments for their harnesses. I figured Ben would be fine, snoozing in the truck, as its AC was ice cold. Sully, a bundle of part-Chihuahua nerves, wasn't going to be a happy camper no matter what. I gave him a double dose of herbal calming medication and briefly considered downing one myself.

We had about 22 plastic bins, a wardrobe moving box, 5 regular cardboard boxes, and miscellaneous items, like my stationary bike, folding tables and our gas grill to cram into the utility trailer. Duffle bags with clothes for the trip, along with a cooler of drinks, dog food and other dog-related items, would ride in the Prius.

The two plastic storage sheds that housed tools and other outdoor items had been taken apart by my old man, and would be strapped in the bed of the truck over the tops of even more plastic bins.

He'd also dismantled the wooden steps and small porch he'd built in front of the trailer door, and had neatly stacked the lumber at the side of our site. As was the custom, we'd be leaving it behind for park scavengers.

After I finished attending to Ben and Sully's needs and defrosting the fridge, I went outside. It was still early, but already hot and windy, I felt physically drained from long days of packing and getting ready for the trip.

My shoulders and back were sore from hoisting bins around, and my eyes were watery and stinging. I sat in our one remaining folding lawn chair and went over a list of last-minute chores we needed to do.

I was getting a little rattled that we weren't going to be able to fit everything in the vehicles and UHaul, when Lonnie May - minus Daisy May - walked up.

Lonnie seemed uncommonly cheerful. He took off his grimy red tractor hat, wiped it across his even grimier face, and put it back on his head, adjusting the filthy visor over his piggish eyes.

"This-here's your last day, ain't it?"

I nodded. "Yep. We're planning to pull out before noon if we can."

"Welp, I sure hope you guys have a good trip. I tell you what - I'd be out of this shithole park in a flash if it wasn't for my obligations."

I had no idea what he was talking about. The only "obligation" Lonnie had was walking Daisy May around the park so she could crap at somebody else's site, which *obliged them* to clean up after her. He went over and took a seat atop the stack of porch lumber.

"I sure could use this excellent wood," he observed. "I been thinkin' about buildin' a porch for my rig, and this would fill the bill just perfect. How much you askin' for it?"

I knew darn well Lonnie was aware of the Trailer Park Scavenger Law, because he was *always* the first to poke through anything left behind by departing guests or residents, claiming the best items for himself.

What I couldn't figure out was why he was even asking about the lumber, since his trailer was parked right across the street from ours and he would have instant access to it as soon as we pulled out.

I was hot, tired, and dust was blowing into my eyes from the abandoned Cornhole Court. I felt like extracting some payback for all the crap we'd put with out of Lonnie for the past two years, so I twisted the knife. Just a little.

"My old man said the lumber's worth $50 - at least," I lied, waiting for his reaction. He nearly rolled over backwards.

"Whoa there..." he whooped. "Fifty bucks is a lot of money for a pile of junky wood that nobody's got no use for."

"But Lonnie, you just said it was 'excellent' wood, and it would be perfect for your porch!"

"Not at no 50 dollars it wouldn't. That's nothin' but highway train robbery!"

Without commenting on the muddled metaphor, I offered him an alternative deal. "Tell you what, Lonnie. You've been such a great neighbor and all, we'll let you have the whole pile for $25. How's that for a bargain?"

Lonnie took off his cap again, slapped it against his leg and adjusted his neck until it made a loud, nasty cracking sound that almost caused me to piss myself.

"Now look here," he bawled. "That ain't how things is done around here. When you move out, you leave your lumber for folks that's in need. 'Give unto others as they give unto you.' That's in your Bible. You don't go chargin' 'em for it. That ain't Christian-like."

I couldn't resist plunging the knife a little deeper... "I'm truly sorry if I offended you, Lonnie," I said, my voice dripping with sarcasm. "I had no idea that was the tradition...and you *did* want to know how much we were asking for it," I reminded him.

"I was just bein' polite and all," Lonnie grunted. "I figgered you didn't know the ropes on it or you wouldn't be actin' so high and mighty." I sat back in my chair and pretended to contemplate how to make up for my gross insensitivity.

"Well, I guess you can just have it for free then, Lonnie. In fact, you can start taking the lumber right now if you want, before my old man gets back with the UHaul." Lonnie scratched his arm with the remaining fingers on his hand.

"Now, see, that's kind of a problem for me, right there, what with my legs messed up from the accident an' all. I was thinkin' maybe you and your old man could bring the lumber on over to my place when he gets back."

There it was – the *real* reason Lonnie had come over to ask about the lumber and when we were leaving. He *thought we'd carry it over to his trailer for him*. I bit my lip and fixed him with a cold stare.

My back was in spasms, the day was still young, and we had a 5-hour drive ahead of us after we loaded the UHaul. A voice deep down inside was telling me to breathe, but I could barely hear it for the blood pounding in my ears. My hands were trembling in their desire to wrap themselves around his dirty neck, and every muscle in my body was tensed, ready to pounce.

Lonnie, who'd been staring back at me with his grizzly jaw stuck out in defiance, suddenly slumped his shoulders and dropped his head. When he looked back up after a lengthy pause, I saw genuine fear in his bloodshot eyes. I said not a word and made not a move.

"I could get one of my buddies to move it on over," he conceded in a weak voice. "I reckon you-all got too much on your dish today." He stood slowly, and with a loud sniff, pulled on his grubby cap.

"Welp, I reckon I'll see you-all around," he said, as he turned and slouched back across the street. And that, I hoped, would be the last I ever saw of, or heard from, fucking Lonnie May.

THE MORAL OF THIS STORY

Never look a dead-tired gift horse in the mouth. She just might bite your fucking head off or stomp your sorry ass to death.

5 - ON THE ROAD (YET) AGAIN

As you probably guessed, we didn't get out of The Resort until well after noon. My old man got back with the UHaul trailer around 9am, and we started loading it.

Our stuff wasn't fitting in the trailer no matter how tight we jammed in the bins and boxes and odds 'n ends. We kept putting items aside and futilely rearranging bins in the hope we wouldn't have to leave anything behind, seeing as how most of what we were keeping was items with sentimental attachment.

When my old man said we might have to give up one of the dogs if we didn't pare down, I compromised by sacrificing one of my 3 bins of lidless Tupperware, but only on the condition that he'd toss out 3 bins of his stupid car magazines dating back to 1978.

AUTHOR'S NOTE: My willingness to compromise on important issues like this is precisely why our marriage has endured many storms, and has survived many instances of food poisoning due to improperly stored meats and what have you.

The last item we put into the back of the UHaul was my stationary bike. I had two of the damn things. The duplication error was due to my having forgotten I already had one of the damn things. I had accidentally bought it when I joined Weight Watchers after Oprah tricked me into thinking I would actually give up box wine and start exercising just to lose forty lousy pounds.

When I wised up to the scam, I donated the spare bike to Rosie's Thrift Shop, mainly because I couldn't find a sucker at The Resort who would take it for free. I kept the second bike in our storage unit in case Oprah, or Marie Osmond, or some other ex-fatass celebrity ever tricked me into trying to lose weight again. In my mind, the bike was cheap insurance.

At 1:30pm, my old man crammed the bike in at the very back of the trailer, and I leaned against the double doors to keep them closed while he padlocked them.

We stopped at The Resort's office and gave the 5th wheel's door key to Laurette Lopp to give to Gerald Karn. Laurette hugged us both and wished us well, and then we were off, leaving behind over two years of living in a trailer park to head north to live in another trailer park.

It felt good to be leaving The Resort. Despite the fact that all of the park residents were more or less in the same financial boat, me and my old man were sickened at the right-wing extremism and callousness we'd witnessed there.

During two-plus years, not one day had passed without one or more of our neighbors starting a conversation with a hateful remark about Obama and his family, complaining about "illegals," or excoriating "goddamn stupid libruls." They never seemed to give a thought as to whether *we* might be two of the "goddamn stupid libruls" they were ranting about.

My old man had supported Bernie Sanders during the primaries, while I was for Hillary Clinton. Although he'd gotten away with wearing his Bernie T shirt in the park now and then, I hadn't dared to even mention Hillary's name out loud, so hostile was the ginned-up hatred for her, even among people we considered fairly sane.

After the election was over and Trump was inaugurated, her vilification continued, with Trumpists gloating over her "crushing" defeat. They ignored the fact that Hillary had won the popular vote by the widest margin of a losing candidate for president in the history of the United States. They could not be gracious, not even in victory.

We'd worked hard to patch our lives and our savaged savings account back together after devastating personal and financial losses, and we were more than ready to get back to where we once belonged – the Pacific Northwest - or as my late mother-in-law called it: "God's Country."

We pulled out of The Resort full of high hopes, great expectations, and two dogs that had to shit after five minutes on the road.

Two hundred and fifty miles and 10 rest stops later, we arrived at our destination for the night. Unfortunately, so had many other weekend travelers – it was a Friday – and none of the motels near town had a vacancy - or so the desk clerks claimed after listening to Ben and Sully screech-bark from the truck and car.

We drove on, and came to a Motel 6 just off the highway. We were too exhausted to track down a better roost, so we took a room on the ground floor, with two lumpy double beds and something under the desk that Sully found extremely tasty. Whatever it was, it was also very crunchy. The room was supposed to have a microwave and a mini-fridge, but it had neither.

I fed the boys, grabbed a couple artisan-crafted boloney sandwiches from the cooler, ripped open a bag of chips, unscrewed the spigot on the wine box, and we settled in for the night.

The couple occupying the room above ours was practicing for a stomp dancing competition somewhere in the state, and they clomped and thumped until my old man had to get down on his knees and appeal to my Christian charity to save them both from certain death.

The next morning, we left the motel at first light, stopping at a McDonald's on the way out of town, because even though they leave the light on for customers, Motel 6 doesn't offer so much as a wormy apple for breakfast. We entered the freeway on a cheesy, fried egg-and-sausage high, bound for our next stop somewhere in California – God willin' and Ben didn't shit in the truck.

At noon, my old man called ahead and made reservations at a La Quinta Inn we'd found on the internet the night before during a lull in the stomp dance practice. The hotel advertised a Jacuzzi and heated indoor pool, two features that sounded paradisiacal after a night spent trying to fall asleep in a drafty barn during a Native American-sponsored hootenanny.

At the California state line, we pulled up to an agricultural station, where inspectors were checking vehicles to make sure no quarantined plants or exotic invasive species were being brought into the Golden State.

We'd passed through California for the first time decades before, carrying a pretty heavy load of a certain dried plant specimen we'd obtained illegally from a stoner relative back east.

Young, naive, and wary of law enforcement, we'd panicked a half-mile from the inspection station and had dumped our stash, certain we'd be busted by the pigs and locked away in prison for the rest of our lives.

Seeing as how we were both white and were driving a brand new Mazda RX-7 at the time, we should have known better than to think we'd merit suspicion of any kind. Since that experience, we'd stopped at California Agricultural Inspection stations many times, and had never even had to slow down before being waved through.

My old man, driving our truck and pulling the UHaul, was just ahead of me in the line of vehicles, and when it was his turn to pull forward, I saw the inspector walk up to the truck, say something, then step back quickly.

My old man hopped out, closed the door, and headed to the back of the UHaul, followed by the inspector. Ben, alarmed by the sudden disruption to his nap, stuck his head out the open truck window and began screech-barking, which caused Sully to join in the protest with his screeches of his own.

The inspector looked none too pleased with the din coming from both of our vehicles, and as my old man fumbled to find the right key to the padlock on the trailer door, I could see waves of heat rising from the pavement around them both.

I felt relatively safe at that point, because California pot laws had changed significantly since our first state line encounter, and anyway, our stash was buried in the duffle bag Sully was standing on in the back seat.

I figured that even if my old man got sent to the slammer for something the inspector found in the U-Haul, at the very least I'd have a couple weeks' worth of herbage to tide me over until I made it to Oceanview, where weed possession was now legal.

After a lot of juggling and fiddling, my old man finally located the correct key, and undid the padlock on the trailer doors. As they opened, my stationary bike, which had somehow been pushed forward by the shifting bins behind it, came tumbling out.

The inspector and my old man leapt backward just in time to avoid being struck by the rampaging exercise equipment. The inspector glanced, first at the bike, then briefly inside the trailer. Satisfied there was no space left inside the UHaul for invasive plants or anything else, he turned and walked briskly back to his booth.

I could tell my old man was furious. He picked up the bike, angrily shoved it back in the UHaul, and held the doors shut with one shoulder while he re-fastened the padlock. He got back in the truck, started the engine and raced off in a huff. I pulled forward, and the chagrinned inspector waved me on without even looking up.

Our second day on the road was almost twice as long as our first, and by the time we reached the La Quinta it was after dark. I took Ben and Sully for a brief crap/pee walk while my old man checked us in, and we went directly to our room, turned on the air conditioner full blast, and collapsed on the bed.

After a brief rest, my old man brought in our duffels and the dogs' suitcase, which contained their various snacks, treats and toys. I turned on the TV and cracked open our second box of road wine.

My old man donned his swimming trunks and flip flops, and headed for the motel's hot tub and indoor pool. He was back in two minutes and ominously bone dry.

"Wassup?" I solicitously inquired.

"The pool and the Jacuzzi are closed for repairs," he growled, his lower lip trembling ever so slightly. I'd never seen his ears quite so red, and I figured his BP must be somewhere in the 500 range.

I knew I had to do something to prevent a stroke, and damn fast - before the commercials were over and my favorite show, *Better Call Saul,* came back on. It was clearly a matter of life and death.

"Have a glass of wine and relax," I reasoned with him. "*Better Call Saul* is on, and anyway, you can go soak your head in a nice hot bath when it's over. Then, tomorrow you can get online and give this place a really bad review, or call the front desk and whine at the manager."

My old man grudgingly accepted the advice. He pulled on a sweatshirt, drew himself a full plastic glass of wine from the box, and plopped down on the bed next to me and the dogs.

The episode of **Better Call Saul** was a good one. Even though the creepy geezer with the oversized head who played Mike Ehrmantrout sort of reminded me of my old man, and could easily play his part if I ever made the **Trailer Dogs** movie.

I had become infatuated with the fictitious character "Gus Fring," a calm and gentlemanly meth dealer, and owner of a chain of chicken joints in New Mexico - ever since I first saw him on **Breaking Bad**. "Gus" was played by Giancarlo Esposito, whom I found quite attractive in a super-cool Obama sort of way.

I had originally decided on Kevin Spacey to take on the part of my old man, but now I could *definitely* see Esposito in the role, and I made a mental note to contact his agent in the near future.

Spacey's agent had, on several occasions, threatened to report me to the authorities if I didn't stop sexually harassing his client, and I had long since given up on signing him for the movie. And since I'd decided to play myself in the film, I should have a co-star I could really relate to.

When **Better Call Saul** was over, my old man fished clean underwear out of his duffel bag and went in to soak in the bath tub. I heard the bathroom door close, followed by a loud *"Fucking son-of-a-bitch."*

I could not imagine what the problem might be, and to be completely truthful, I was still busy contemplating the many charms of Giancarlo Esposito to care. My old man's Ehrmantrout-size head peered out from the bathroom doorway.

"There's no bathtub in this fucking room – just a walk-in shower."

I hadn't noticed the deficiency when I'd used the bathroom earlier, and try as I might, I could not think of a single answer to this horrendous lack of customer service on the part of La Quinta. "What would Gus Fring do?" I asked myself.

It occurred to me that Gus wasn't the type of guy who would stay at a La Quinta in the first place, and if he *did* book a room in one, it would probably be only for an hour or two so he could cement a drug deal.

I sure as hell couldn't see Gus spending the night in anything less than a Hilton, and I suspected that he would send the homely, but *extremely* efficient Ehrmantrout on a mission to extract revenge for La Quinta's double-cross. I felt certain I had stumbled upon the perfect solution...

Early the next morning I explained his avenging mission to my old man. Afterwards, I removed the ice bucket and plastic glasses from a tray on top of the mini-fridge cabinet, and handed the tray to him.

He was to take the tray to La Quinta's breakfast room and bring back 4 coffees, two bowls of cereal, 2 cartons of 2% skimmed milk (1% would have been ok, but I didn't want any fat-free), and 4 pieces of thickly buttered toast.

I wrote the order down just in case he got there and forgot where he was and what he was supposed to do, like he often did in bed.

To my astonishment, he carried out the assignment to perfection, and returned to our room with the items on my list, plus several small cups of strawberry jam for the toast, two crispy waffles, and a packet of syrup.

After we finished eating, I emptied the contents of my old man's duffel bag into the dogs' suitcase and sent him back to the breakfast room with instructions to fill the bag with as many sweet rolls as he could get his hands on, *and* without attracting attention from any guests who might be lingering over their morning coffee.

If he *did* encounter an overly observant breakfaster, well, we would find a way to deal with the gringo later.

When he got back to the room I had everything packed and ready to go. His duffel bag was bulging with wrapped muffins of all artificial flavors, sweet rolls bursting with lemon, strawberry and apple centers, apples, bananas, oranges, and 5 cups of premium yogurt. He'd even remembered to pilfer paper napkins and spoons for the yogurt.

Despite his resemblance to the monstrous Ehrmantrout, I was prouder of him at that moment than I ever had been before. I leashed up the boys and took them out to the parking lot for their morning craps while he loaded the Prius. Then we were off on the next lap of our journey to Oceanview.

Somewhere around Sacramento, I began to notice how uncharacteristically quiet Sully was in the back seat, except for an occasional scratching and scuffling noise, which I attributed to him re-arranging his stink blanket in a more comfortable configuration.

Nonetheless, I used the walkie talkie to contact my old man in the truck ahead, and told him we needed to pull off at the next exit to have a snack and walk the boys.

We exited onto a country road with a wide shoulder, and while he took Ben and Sully for a short walk, I opened the hatch of the Prius and looked around. I didn't notice the big wet stain on the side of the flattened duffel bag, but when I unzipped it, the pungent odor of probiotics and sweet rolls floored me.

Somehow or another, through a combination of digging and repeated pouncing on the duffel, Sully had managed to force the tops off several of the yogurts, which had leaked all over the bag. Thumbless, and therefore not equipped to unzip the duffel, he'd continued to knead and scratch until his persistence reduced the sweet rolls and muffins, still in their packages, to crumbs.

Some of the packages had split open and pulverized crumbs had mixed with yogurt liquid, forming a soupy batter-like mess in and around the apples, bananas and oranges my old man had pilfered from the motel's breakfast room. He had carelessly forgotten to put the yogurts in a separate cooler, a fuck up of massive proportions and grave consequences for the cartel.

One thing was perfectly clear: Both of us were way too lazy to clean up the mess. At the next rest stop we tossed the duffel bag and its gloppy contents into the nearest trash can, and raced back onto the freeway.

My debriefing of Ehrmantrout's failed mission was going to have to wait until we decamped at the next La Quinta. Or Motel 6, depending on traffic and the number of shit stops we had to make for Ben.

Late in the afternoon we reached our next destination much earlier than we'd thought possible. We checked into a small, generic roadside motel next door to a Mexican restaurant. After feeding Ben and Sully and supplying them with ample chew sticks, we walked over to the cantina to have an early dinner.

The place was empty except for us. While we waited for my chili rellenos and his jumbo burrito, my old man took out a pen and turned over his paper placemat to figure out how in the hell we'd made such good time on the road. He was well into his mathematical calculations when I noticed the clock on the wall.

According to everything I'd been taught about telling time, it was only 2pm. It appeared that, in addition to his abject failure with the duffel bag caper, Ehrmantrout had failed to account for the time difference at The Resort and in California.

Fortunately, his mistake didn't dull our appetites. We cleaned our platas and two baskets of chipitas, and washed them down with fishbowl- size margaritas. We walked back to the motel with the confidence of two bloated gringos who knew there was a package of Gas X tucked away in the dogs' suitcasita.

In the motel's parking lot, we noticed two Latinas standing next to an ancient sedan near the open door to one of the motel rooms. The women were comforting two small, curly-coated dogs, whose heads were hanging out the passenger side window. In the doorway of the motel room, two young children, a boy and a girl, appeared to be distress.

"What do you suppose that's about?" I wondered aloud.

"God only knows," my old man replied, fishing for the card key, which he'd obviously left on the desk inside the room.

Ben and Sully heard us fumbling at the door and started to raise ten kinds of hell. My old man took off to the motel office for a pass key, and I waited for him, still watching the drama unfold in the parking lot, and trying, unsuccessfully, to get Ben and Sully to STFU.

When he got back with the pass key card, my old man related the story. The two Latinas had checked into the motel sometime after we had, and had barely been able to afford a room for the night, which they'd paid for in cash. The motel's manager watched them as they carried their luggage into the room, and then saw them come back for the two little dogs.

"Guess the beaners thought they could get away without paying the $20 pet fee," he'd told my old man. "They asked if they could have a refund and go someplace else, but their kids already used the toilet, and I said 'no way, José'. Their dogs are just going to have to spend the night in the car."

I didn't need to hear any more. While my old man went into our room to quiet Ben and Sully, I stormed over to the motel office, marched up to the counter and slapped a twenty dollar bill down. The manager was sitting behind the counter, thumbing through a magazine and drinking coffee.

"Here's for the *beaners'* dogs to stay in your shithole room," I said matter-of-factly. He looked up at me with his ugly mouth hanging open, but didn't say anything. I was so fucking mad, I almost knocked over a chair on my way out the door.

I went over to the womens' car and told them it was ok for them to take their dogs inside, that the manager had made a mistake about the pet fee. They were overwhelmed with relief. I glanced inside their car, and it looked like everything they owned was in there.

With a heavy accent and gestures, one of them told me the car door didn't lock and the window wouldn't go all the way up. That was why they were afraid to leave their dogs alone in there all night.

They had been prepared to take shifts sleeping in the car with the dogs. I understood completely.

No matter where you're from or what your station in life, the love of dogs is universal, even in certain areas of Asia, where they're often an entrée on the menu. The next morning when we got up, the Latinas, their two kids and the dogs were gone.

Our fourth day on the road was fairly uneventful and mostly boring, except when we stopped for soft serve at a Dairy Queen and Ben took the whole fucking top off my cone after being offered one lick. I cleaned up his muzzle with a wad of napkins, and we soldiered on.

That night we stayed at a kind of fancy Best Western Inn that had its own dog walk, equipped with free plastic poop bags.

In celebration of our last night on the road in a motel with free dog shit bags, an indoor pool and hot tub, we opened wine from a real bottle and ordered a deluxe pie from a nearby pizza place. Three hours and 3 joints later, we remembered the pizza hadn't been delivered.

My old man got on the horn to the pizza parlor and was told they'd never received our order. Too stoned to argue and not sure he'd even called the right place, he hung up, grabbed a fistful of cash and went down the hall to the snack-vending machine.

When he got back, we dined on thirty bucks' worth of Snickers, Doritos, Corn Nuts, Reeses Cups and Peanut M&Ms, after which he remembered the inn's functioning pool and hot tub near the lobby.

He put on his trunks & flip flops, grabbed a towel, and off he went in search of nirvana. He was back in 5 minutes, madder than hell. It was after 10pm, and the pool and hot tub were closed.

We wearily fired up another cone, scarfed down the last of the M&Ms, and fell asleep to the sound of rain pounding on the patio outside our room.

When we'd left The Resort, temperatures were in the 90's, and we were dressed in shorts and T-shirts. I was wearing sandals. Now we'd need to scrounge up long pants and hoodies, and I'd have to trade my sandals for socks and sneakers.

We weren't even to Oceanview yet, and already we were **FREEZING. OUR. BALLS. OFF.** My balls had disappeared entirely, and my old man's balls appeared to be hanging by a thread. Balls or no balls, *still we persisted*.

THE MORAL OF THIS STORY

Before traveling north from the desert, be sure to stock up on warm clothing, snacks, and a shitload of weed. And if you're traveling with dogs and can't afford to stay at fancy schmancy motels, don't forget to bring your own shit bags. And one more thing: If you ever unilaterally decide to separate a mother from her dogs or her kids, and I happen to be around to see it, you better call fucking Saul.

6 - SASQUATCH STAN

In the late afternoon on day four of our travels, we reached Oceanview. It was cold and foggy, and the battery in our community gate opener was dead, so we called the maintenance office to send someone to let us in.

When we pulled up to our lot, I was relieved to see that the 5th wheel and travel trailer were just as we'd left them, except that the tarp on the big trailer had blown partly off.

Weeds had grown up around both trailers and under them and everywhere else in the yard. As my old man gratefully observed, it was *way too* wet and soggy for him to use a weed whacker.

We went inside the travel trailer first. The dehumidifier, which was still humming away, had worked perfectly. Everything was dry, and no more mushrooms had sprouted along the walls. We plugged in a space heater and left Ben and Sully curled up on the couch while we checked out the 5th wheel. At first glance everything looked ok.

The carpet in the living area was stained and grimy as it had been after we took possession and Truth and Strength had removed the area rug they'd used to cover it up.

The interior smelled sort of musty, like anything that had been closed up for four months during a constant downpour. It wasn't until we pulled the sofa bed out from the wall of a slide-out in the living room that we noticed *considerable* dampness along the baseboard.

Whether it had come from the slide-out's roof or from around the window, we really couldn't tell. We would have to deal with it later. There was too much to unload and I was too punchy with fatigue to even start the process of blaming my old man for the haste and impatience that had resulted in our buying the rolling money pit.

We switched on the electric fireplace to warm the place up, and I began carrying in bins and unloading them while my old man turned on the water at the main line and fiddled with our internet connections.

I'd just hoisted a bin full of clothes out of the truck, when a grizzled old guy appeared from out of the heavy mist. He was dressed in rumpled camouflage and walked with a very pronounced limp.

Upon closer examination, I noted that one of his feet was prosthetic, and was shod in a gigantic black dress shoe. His other foot was encased in a military-style boot.

"Hey there," he grunted. "Y'all new around here?" I told him we'd just arrived from the southwest and were moving our stuff into the 5th wheel. I sort of hoped he'd take a hint and go away so I could finish unloading, but he leaned up against the truck and pulled out a pack of unfiltered cigarettes.

Lighting one, he inhaled deeply, blowing a stream of smoke in my direction. He acted as though he had all the time in the world and was ready to share it with lucky me.

"Well, welcome to the neighborhood. I'm Stan Carlyle. Me and my old lady live over there in that trailer," he said, waving an arm toward a dilapidated rig that was kitty-corner across the road.

The side of the trailer had streaks of green mold on it, and a blue tarp was stretched across the front. A Trump-Pence sign stood cock-eyed at the side of the trailer, and in the front was a gaggle of small, faded American flags in various stages of decay.

"In the winter we haul ass to BLM land in Arizona and live on the cheap," he said, as if to explain the up-scale accommodations they were now enjoying in the moldering trailer.

"We just got in last week. Ain't had time to clean up." I nodded, but didn't say anything, not wishing to invite further conversation in my weary state. Stan apparently took my reticence as an invitation to continue a one-sided dialogue.

"I got me a shop out back there," he continued, spitting a shred of loose tobacco out the side of his mouth. "Built it right after we moved in here. That was 15 years ago. It's fallin' apart now, but I got my tools in there, and my old lady keeps her crafts in it. She's crippled up with arthritis and don't get out much."

Based on his age, the camouflage outfit, the prosthetic foot, and all the US flags, I speculated Stan might be a Vietnam vet – perhaps a wounded warrior. He seemed to read my mind.

"This foot ain't real," he informed me, presenting the huge prosthetic for inspection. "I got myself in a huntin' accident back when I was drinkin' hard. Blew half my own goddamn foot off. Docs had to take a saw to the rest of her. Don't slow me down much anymore."

In spite of my exhaustion, I was transfixed. Not so much with Stan as he now stood before me, but at the real possibility we had entered the *Twilight Zone*, and an evil, mutant robot, part Lonnie May and part Cripple John, was living across the street from us.

"You don't happen to own an Australian Heeler named Daisy May do you, Stan?" I asked, fearing what his answer might be.

"Naw…naw…never had no use for dogs," he snorted, and I breathed a sigh of relief.

"Had me a Maine Coon, though. Big old cat named Willie. Meanest goddamn thing you ever saw. He was like a attack cat or some such shit. Just as soon claw your ass to shreds as look at ya. My old lady hated him. Wouldn't let the sum-bitch inside the trailer. He slept out in the shop in bad weather. Got into her stuff one day and tore up a bunch of her craft shit."

Stan laughed heartily at the memory. Then he got a sober look on his face. "Somebody ran ol' Willie down in the street about 8 years back. I miss the brute sometimes…" He brushed a tear from his eye, looked away, and took another drag from his cig. The Lonnie May vibe was so strong, it was sending shock waves through my body. It began to drizzle, and I was chilled and feeling slightly woozy.

"Well, I need to get back to work and get these bins in the trailer," I said, with a trace of 'get your ass off my property and leave me the fuck alone' in my voice. Stan didn't notice my cue, and the similarity to my first encounter with Lonnie May deepened.

"The gal that lived in your spot ten years ago up and moved to Alaska. She was a good old gal – a real pisser. Used to have us over for drinks ever now and then," he said, raising one eyebrow and glancing at me hopefully. I didn't respond. "She had a flar garden over by where you got that dinky trailer parked..."

Stan seemed to momentarily lose his train of thought, and his gravelly voice trailed off. I hoped it might be the sign of an impending fatal heart attack, but then he picked up again on a completely different tack.

"Got me good neighbors on either side now. Don't complain about *nothin'*. Before, I had that asshole Tom Kelly next door. Belly-ached all the time about my yard and me parkin' my truck in his spot an' all. I couldn't leave a goddamn transmission out in the yard for a week without him bitchin' to management about it."

Stan stubbed out the butt of his cigarette and pulled another one from a crumpled pack.

"Ever week Kelly was callin' the health department on me, or gettin' his ass in the air over some damn thing. Bastard threatened to sue me onct, and I said to him, I says, 'Tom, you by God do what you have to do, and I'll do by God what I have to do, and we'll see who comes out on top.' He put his place up for sale not too long after that. I always figured he was the one who ran Willie down, but I couldn't prove it in a court a law."

Rain was dripping off the bill of Stan's cap and I was shivering in the cold. The water was collecting in my eyebrows and rolling into my eyes, combining with the actual salty tears I was now shedding. Stan was oblivious to my suffering.

"How much did y'all pay for your lot?" he demanded. I shrugged and shook my head, wishing the clouds would part and a bolt of lightning would strike us both dead. When I didn't answer, he barged right on.

"Well, I reckon we paid a lot less for our spot than you did for yours. Lots in here is goin' for 10 times what we paid back in the day, and there ain't no blacks or Mexicans in here to drive the values down. You got yourself a big one, so you probbly got took for even more!" he chortled.

"I reckon if we was to up and sell our place, we'd be rollin' in dough. And with ol' Trump runnin' the show now instead of dumb-ass Obama, the economics is goin' to get even better for us white folks."

I was too numb with cold and loathing to comment. Then a loud rapping noise got my attention. It wasn't the lightning strike I'd hoped for, but it interrupted Stan's racist soliloquy. He glanced over towards his trailer.

"That's my old lady bangin' her cane on the wall. I better go see what the hell she wants now. It's always somethin' with you damn women."

With that, he clomped off, favoring his enormous foot and pausing to flick his cigarette butt into the bushes. Without a trace of remorse, I wished ol' Tom Kelly had been there to run his ass down.

I lifted the heavy bin and carried it inside the trailer. Then I sank into the recliner nearest to the electric fireplace. My old man came in from hooking up the water and internet.

"We can't live here," I stated flatly, drained of all emotion and robbed of the will to live.

"For God's sake – we just got here. We'll settle in, wait and see. Hey - who was the old guy with the giant foot you were talking to?"

"It was fucking Lonnie May, and this is The Resort, only in a tidal marsh. We can't live here," I repeated.

"Oh, come on now – it isn't *that* bad," my old man cajoled. "You're just tired and need a good hot shower to relax you."

He went over and flipped the switch to turn on the water heater. It didn't light. He flipped it again, and it still didn't light. He went back outside and checked the propane tank. It was full, and all the connections were tight. He came in and flipped the switch again. It didn't light.

Finally, he sat down at the computer and ordered a new water heater, all the time cursing Lyin' Truth for the con job she'd pulled on him about the condition of the 5th wheel.

Enthusiastically supportive of my old man's display of self-loathing and guilt, I scrounged up the last of our weed stash from my unpacked duffel. An hour later we hit the sack, dirty, and stuffed to the gills with store-bought chips and watery guacamole.

Sure, we might be stuck in the middle of a fucking rain forest in a leaky trailer full of broken down appliances, mildewed carpet, and mushrooms sprouting from the baseboards, but at least we weren't Trump-loving, name-calling dupes like our jackass neighbor, Stan "Big Foot" Carlyle.

THE MORAL OF THIS STORY

Fools take no delight in understanding, but only in displaying what they think. Proverbs 18:2, as tweeted by Senator "Liddle Marco" Rubio, Oct. 18, 2017.

7 - PROJECTS

My old man is never so happy as when chaos is all around him and shit's hitting the fan left and right. In fact, he's usually the one shitting and then turning the fan on. He's the kind of guy who starts five projects at the same time, half-finishes all five, and then starts five more.

I can't even trust my old man to give the dogs a bath. He's been known to put shampoo on their heads and then some POS movie comes on TV, and he leaves them in the tub with soap in their eyes for the next two hours while he watches *Twilight* for the umpteenth time.

He will WATCH ANYTHING on TV, no matter how crappy it is – hell, even if Adam Sandler's in it - and *especially* if it's about a conniving husband plotting to kill his wife. He was utterly transfixed by the O.J. Simpson movie, to the extent I threw out all our kitchen knives and hid his leather gloves.

I forgot to add that when he engages in one of his simultaneous multiple projects, my old man whines and complains and throws his tools around from start to half-completion. Sometimes a screw driver or a hand saw he was using to adjust a gate will be unearthed years later, and the gate will still be hanging by one screw. It has happened.

Anyways, about a week after our inauspicious arrival at Oceanview, and after he'd managed to almost complete the installation of the new water heater, he set to work writing up a list of projects and items that needed replacement. It was a looooong one.

First on the list was buying an electric fireplace to replace the one that had stopped working our second night in the trailer. Other items on the list were as follows:

- Replace toilet with one that holds water

- Replace propane stove with an oven that lights and doesn't have 10 years of sludge build up that Truth didn't clean off with fucking vinegar.

- Replace vent hood over stove with a vent that has a working fan

- Replace microwave with a microwave that microwaves

- Replace ceiling hatches with hatches that don't have cracks and don't leak around the edges

- Caulk all leaky windows and roof seams

- Track down mildewy smell coming from vicinity of carpet throughout the trailer

- Replace carpet throughout trailer with vinyl flooring

- Replace king mattress with one that doesn't smell bad and has dust mites

- Replace sofa with one that doesn't smell bad and has dust mites

- Track down mildewy smell coming from around windows

- Replace window blinds with ones that don't smell like mildew and have dust mites

- Remove non-working stacked washer & dryer from utility closet and replace rotted flooring; dispose of washer & dryer

- Remove tattered awning, track down Truth and Strength, and shove it up their asses

The list was to be heavily supplemented over the next few weeks with other repairs and replacements, large and small. It didn't include bigger projects, like:

- Demolish rotting garden shed/boardwalk and haul them off

- Build a utility shed with a flush toilet and sink and room for a regular size washer & dryer

- Construct a covered deck and "boardwalk" to keep us dry when going to and from the laundry shed on rainy days (i.e., every day)

- Landscape lot and put in a graveled parking area

- Build a large enough shed where old man can do his computer work, putter around with his hobbies, and leave me the hell alone during the day *(Until that could be done, he'd set up an office in the small travel trailer.)*

Had the mildewy smell in the trailer's carpet not been so offensive, I might have moved the construction of my old man's old man cave to the top of the to-do list. As it was, we donned masks and began ripping the filthy pelt up.

Sections of the floor's underlayment were ruined from being damp and had to be removed and replaced. While we waited for delivery of new vinyl flooring, we tackled the yard, including hacking back overgrown vines and weeds that had invaded both sides of the lot.

One afternoon, while raking up a particularly thick accumulation of decomposed vegetation, I inadvertently exposed numerous artifacts, which, in trailer park vernacular, very nearly caused me to "fill my pants."

So unexpected and unnerving was the discovery, its authenticity would have challenged the belief of my most ardent fans had I not possessed a camera and the journalistic skills to submit the remarkable story to the community's *Marketplace Weekly Mailer:*

FOR IMMEDIATE PUBLICATION

Dateline: Oceanview RV Trailer Resort

Ancient Canadian Corn Holing Grounds Un-earthed in Local Trailer Park

Scientists from all four corners of the globe are heralding/herrolding/geraldoing (sp?) the awesomeness of an awesome discovery made by a newly-minted female resident of Oceanview, the county's premier trailer park.

While digging up weeds and other shit from the far boundaries of her property, the adventuresome lass uncovered awesome ruins from a prehistoric Cornhole Court used by primitive societies, such as Canadians, who appear to have inhabited the site long before anybody could write things down or prove whether they were really Canadians or not.

Anyways, while many modern-day Canadians have long denied a taste for, or interest in corn holing, other more honest persons of Canadian extraction have admitted a fondness for the ungodly sport, and have apologized profusely for their country's lingering obsession with its widespread practice.

The priceless ruins, as I am re-mentioning for readers who weren't paying attention a minute ago, are believed to have been part of a crude Cornhole Court, constructed by marauding Canadian mongrels who occupied the Oceanview RV Trailer Park before they were ruthlessly driven out by Native American mongrels, who were driven out by ruthless European mongrels, who were driven out by ruthless Immigrant mongrels, who were driven out by ruthless white trash, who were driven out by ruthless Russian mongrels in early 2017.

Anyways, in a photograph taken by the female personage who made the awesome and valuable find, *"Product of Canada"* is clearly visible, and is etched into a brick-like paving stone often used in ancient Cornhole Court structures of this type.

Surrounding the relic were numerous dried corn cobs, or "organic hole-pokers" as they are often described in Canadian lore. The cobs somehow survived centuries, perhaps even decades, of really bad fucking weather and remorseless usage.

Persons interested in acquiring the highly collectible and valuable relics should consult Page 23 of *The Marketplace Weekly Mailer*, under the heading: *Items for Sale*. All offers considered. (Will consider trade for functioning water bong.) ###

Canadian Sports Relic Unearthed in Local Trailer Park

AUTHOR'S NOTE: I regret to inform readers that my submission to
The Marketplace Weekly Mailer was never published, due
primarily, I suspect, to the calculated suppression of facts about the
region's shameful past.

And while I'm on the subject, Marketplace Weekly also blatantly
engaged in the dissemination of FAKE NEWS, particularly as
concerned crowd size at the annual "Miss Oyster Pageant and
Coronation," which was attended by 15, not 12 people, as reported.
Concerned citizens may protest these injustices by writing "Return
to Sender" on the front of the mailer and dropping it in the nearest
mail box, or by not picking one up from the FREE rack at the
entrance to Safeway.

After we had completed most of the yard work and had demolished and hauled away the rotting garden shed at the back of the lot, it started raining again, and we concentrated on indoor projects.

We replaced the toilet, stove, stove vent fan, and microwave, and my old man drew up plans for a raised, covered deck. We also ordered an 8′ X 12′ shed kit for his future office, and decided to frame in the 9′ X 12′ ramada next to the proposed deck and outfit it with a sink, toilet, washer and dryer.

The park was still relatively empty, Stan Carlyle and his wife (whom I still hadn't met) being the only other neighbors in residence on our street. We hadn't seen much of Stan after my first encounter with him.

Once in a while I spotted him limping down the street toward the office, a cigarette dangling from his mouth and a rolled-up magazine in his hand. I figured he was using the facilities at the clubhouse, maybe out of a sense of olfactory decency, or maybe because his toilet didn't hold water any better than ours had.

Despite the spotty weather, our projects were coming along ok. When the sun was out, living at Oceanview was downright fabulous. Greenbelts between the lots offered privacy, and for the most part, there seemed to be a "live and let live" attitude at the park. No one bothered us.

After a day of strenuous physical labor, we collapsed in our lawn chairs and sat outside, swilling wine from the box and deciding which improvement to tackle next. Ben and Sully sat with us – *on* us, actually - enjoying the fresh air and filtered sunlight, with Sully's big ears tracking each and every slight noise, and Ben snoozing contentedly on my old man's lap.

Finished covered deck

Our relocation was, so far, fairly successful - much better than I'd anticipated. The small community outside the trailer park was laid-back, poorly dressed, and had pretty much everything we needed to get by.

The weather, although too rainy for my tastes, was a damn sight better than broiling inside a trailer at The Resort. We were able to take the dogs on long walks without any of us collapsing with heatstroke in the middle of the street, or the boys frying the pads off their feet on sizzling concrete.

Life was good – very, very good, in fact. Hell, life was almost *great again!*

THE MORAL OF THE STORY

Never count your chickens before they are hatched.

8 - THE CHAPTER I DIDN'T WANT TO WRITE

It was Sunday, and it had started out well enough. We got up early, fed the boys, fixed our bowls of cereal, shared our bowls of cereal with the boys, and drank a pot of coffee. Then we went outside to work in the yard. It was partly cloudy and on the cool side, which was perfect for the task at hand – creating a walkway of crushed rock up to and around the trailer.

We'd bought a load of used bricks from a guy in town and were going to use them to line the sides of the walkway. We'd already leveled a path and laid down weed-preventing cloth, and this morning's chore was to haul several yards of crushed rock from the bed of the truck and spread it over the fabric.

We knew that eventually most of the path would be covered by a planned deck, but we were tired of tracking wet leaves, mud and pine needles into the trailer every time we took the boys out.

The work was back-breaking, but we kept at it, knowing rain was in the afternoon forecast, as usual. Around 2pm we stopped for a bite to eat, and then we both nodded off in our recliners, like you sometimes read about old people doing in books about old people and their strange, unpredictable ways.

We were woken around 3 by the boys, demanding their dinner. Outside, the rain had commenced. My back was aching like an SOB from hauling and spreading gravel, and I was ravenous, having eaten only half of a peanut butter sandwich for lunch.

My old man, being the quick thinker he is, suggested we drive over to the supermarket, pick up a rotisserie chicken and a side of fried spuds, bring our feast back to the trailer, and call it a day. I offered no objection, so we donned our hoodies, put Ben and Sully in the back of the Prius, and set sail.

In the parking lot at the grocery store, I realized I wasn't going to be able to get out of the car. My back had frozen up, and even moving my leg a little sent pain shooting up my spine. Turning left or right did the same, and I winced as I fumbled in my purse for Ibuprofin.

I managed to scratch out a quick shopping list for my old man, and he headed into the store, leaving me and the boys to fend for ourselves while he foraged for dinner.

A minute or two after he left, I heard a loud hacky cough in the back seat. Then another, and another after that. I tried to turn around to see what was happening, but excruciating pain in my back prevented me from doing so.

I reached up and adjusted the rear view mirror for a view of Ben and Sully. Sully was sitting to one side, staring worriedly at Ben, who was half-standing and making noises as though he was trying to clear his throat. I recognized the symptoms immediately from years past. Ben was experiencing heart failure.

Somehow, I managed to extract the phone from the bottom of my purse, but in my panic, I couldn't think of who to call. Instead, I plucked a baby aspirin from my pill stash, and ignoring lightning strikes of back pain, turned around and lifted Ben onto my lap.

I forced the aspirin down his throat and told myself it would help him. By the time my old man got back to the car, however, I was shaking with emotion. "I think this is it," I said, barely able to get the words out. He took one look at me and at Ben, and nodded.

We drove back to the trailer in silence, Ben weak and shivering slightly on my lap, and Sully tense and alert in the back of the car.

For the next three hours we sat on the couch, Ben between us on his blanket as we stroked his back and head, and spoke to him softly, telling him between our sobs that it was ok for him to leave us. Sully laid on the floor at our feet, as down in the dumps as he'd looked the day we first saw him at the shelter.

Ben rose only once again to cough loudly before collapsing on his blanket. His eyes rolled back in his head and he was panting furiously. When his legs began to stretch robotically and the panting mercifully stopped, we knew our sweet Ben had left the building for good.

I removed his collar and wrapped his lifeless little body tightly in the blanket, papoose style. My old man got up and went outside to dig a grave under a pine tree. Sully sniffed at Ben's blanket shroud, and seemed to understand that his best friend and mentor was gone forever.

Outside, I could hear my old man trying to choke off sobs as he dug in the rocky soil at the back of the lot. When he finished, he came inside and picked Ben up, cradling him in his arms. I carried Sully, and the two of us trudged outside in a chilly mist to bury our boy. My old man laid Ben gently in his grave, and we said our final goodbyes.

Back inside, we opened another box of wine, filled water glasses to the brims, and sat on the couch with tears rolling down our cheeks and Sully between us, head on paws. I don't remember how long we sat there in shock.

Around midnight Sully suddenly hopped down from the couch and walked over to Ben's foam day bed. He inspected its center, then stepped back and circled, sniffing intently around the bed's edges. The examination complete, he lifted his hind leg and took a long, thoughtful piss on it.

The King was dead. Long live the King.

THE MORAL OF THE STORY

In return for the tremendous joy a dog will bring into your life, you must ultimately be prepared to accept the tremendous sorrow when they leave you. But you never are.

Sully & Ben

Ben's final resting place under the pine tree

9 - LIFE AFTER DEATH

The week following Ben's death is more or less a blur to me, as I stayed heavily medicated for the pain in my lower back and the even worse pain in my heart. My old man, a computer systems developer, coped by concentrating on work assignments and attending Skype meetings out in the travel trailer.

Sully and I stayed inside the big trailer, over-eating and watching the news. Trump was digging himself in deeper and deeper trouble after firing James Comey. None of it came as a surprise to me at all, and frankly, I wasn't all that interested in the unbelievable mess America had gotten itself into. Ben was dead and that was all that was on my mind.

I started blaming myself for Ben's death almost immediately as I had with every other dog we'd owned.

It didn't matter that Ben was 18 years old and had lived a long, happy, healthy life. I tortured myself, wondering if we should have rushed him to the vet after his weird spell at The Resort, or whether we shouldn't have taken him for walks on warm days, or if the baby aspirin I'd forced down him the afternoon of his heart attack had actually been what did him in.

Looming large over all my feelings of guilt was the 4-day trip from The Resort to Oceanview. What the hell had we been thinking subjecting an old geezer like Ben to a journey like that?

The stress and excitement were obviously what had caused his death. The only thing that distracted me from the irrational, grief-stricken thoughts was the physical pain in my back, and even that didn't seem like punishment enough.

Clouds of depression I'd suffered in 2013, after the deaths of my best friend and two of our dogs, started to close in on me again. The weather at Oceanview had improved dramatically, but I stayed inside the trailer, hiding mostly from the gut-wrenching sight of Ben's grave, which my old man had surrounded with bricks and covered with rocks to discourage squirrels.

I ordered a marker with the phrase *"If love could have saved you, you would have lived forever"* inscribed on it," and when it came, I couldn't take it out of the box. My old man glued Ben's name tag to it and positioned the marker up against the bricks behind his grave.

I knew I was in a bad place emotionally, but I didn't know what to do about it. Worse, I didn't know if I *wanted* to do anything about it. In the end it was Sully who provided the answer.

I was sitting in front of the computer, persecuting myself with scanned pictures of all the dogs we'd loved over the years. There was Bo, our first, a feisty miniature poodle; and Dolly, our second poodle, a toy who'd died at age 7 of a leaky heart valve (misdiagnosed as Kennel Cough by an idiot vet). Then we'd acquired Honey, a pure white toy Yorki-Poo so Bo wouldn't be lonely.

When Bo died at age 16 – the same year my mother-in-law passed away - we adopted her orphaned Lhasa Apso - Poodle mix, Ginger, as a companion for Honey. Honey lived to 17, and when she crossed the so-called rainbow bridge, we got another toy Poodle, Holly, for Ginger's housemate. When Ginger crossed the bridge due to old age, we got puppy Yorki-Poo Ben to console Holly.

Cheekly, our rescue Chihuahua, had been a wild card, after we saw him, starved and with a mouth full of rotten teeth, at a rescue shelter. Cheekly was with us for 7 years when he died unexpectedly of heart failure, caused by years of neglect at a puppy mill.

Two weeks after Cheekly died, and five months shy of her 17th birthday, congestive heart failure finally got the best of her, and the vet said it was Holly's "time."

We were heart-broken at having to let her go, but none of us so much as Ben. Always up for a vigorous game of tug-of-war, he became listless and uninterested in his toys. His appetite flagged too, and that was when I really became concerned.

One dreary morning as I was skimming the website of the rescue organization where we'd adopted Cheekly, I came across a picture of a skinny, forlorn-looking little Chihuahua-Schnauzer mix with an under bite and gigantic ears.

"Pepe" had spent several days on the run in a city neighborhood when he was attacked by a larger dog. Animal Control was called, and Pepe was trapped and taken in. His back was sutured and he was neutered. He was also injected with a Kennel cough vaccine that made him very, very sick.

I'll never know exactly what it was that so attracted me to Pepe, but whatever it was, it was a powerful draw, love at first sight. When my old man got home, I told him we were going to adopt a new dog "for Ben." I called the rescue people and informed them we'd be there the following weekend to claim Pepe. And that's exactly what we did.

The adoption of Sully (as we later re-named him) turned to be the remedy for our despondent, ailing pack. He and Ben bonded immediately, and Ben's appetite and playfulness quickly returned.

Sully was suspicious of me and my old man in the beginning, but when we simply ignored him and made no attempt to grab him, he was soon queuing up behind Ben for treats, and pushing his way onto our laps in the evening. As usually happens with rescues, we were left wondering who really rescued whom.

So, the fateful morning after I'd grieved my way through pictures of our dogs, loved and lost, I went to rescue websites in the Oceanview area and began scanning through their protégés. Sadly, most of the abandoned dogs were pit bulls or pit bull mixes that had been rescued from abusive owners, or simply dumped because of their reputation, undeserved, for overly- aggressive behavior.

There was no question that as badly as I felt for them, we couldn't responsibly take on a dog of that size, and particularly a dog that might need obedience training. Hell, neither one of us could make an 8-pound Poodle obey us. I gave up the quest for the time being and vowed to widen my search the next day.

The next morning I found an adorable little female terrier mix at a rescue shelter not too far away. She was 15 lbs - larger than Sully - but approximately his age, which we estimated at 6 or 7 years. Cindy been surrendered by an elderly owner who could no longer care for her, and was being fostered until she could be placed.

Cindy was described as loving and playful, spayed and in good health. I called the number of the shelter and was told that her foster parents had decided to keep her. I found two other possibilities later in the day, but both dogs had already been spoken for when I called.

I gave up and turned on the news, hoping to hear that Trump had resigned. My disappointment increased tenfold when I learned that he had not. That afternoon I received an email from my old man, who was working out in the travel trailer, and who'd been browsing the rescue sites himself: *"Take a look at this one. Me like."*

I clicked on the link, which was from a rescue organization about an hour and a half drive from Oceanview, and up popped a picture of a small white female dog. She was facing the camera straight on, and a shaggy white top knot all but concealed her eyes. A large black nose protruded from a fluffy muzzle.

According to the write-up, two years previously "Pixie" been taken in as a puppy stray, along with her mother. Both dogs had been adopted, but by different families. Pixie was placed with a family who later moved and could not take her with them, and an elderly, well-intentioned neighbor had taken her in.

Unfortunately, for the rambunctious Pixie, the neighbor's older and larger dog was jealous of the playful newcomer. Weeks later it had attacked her, viciously ripping open the left side of her chest and back. The neighbor took Pixie to a vet and had her stitched up, and then returned her to the original rescue organization, explaining tearfully that her home was not safe for the little dog.

The rescuers took Pixie in, had her now-infected sutures treated at a vet, and paid for her spaying. It was noticeable in the picture that the fur around Pixie's wounds had not yet grown back in after being shaved, and she had red scars along her chest and back from the attack.

She was being fostered by a local couple, but after a six weeks with them she was deemed fit for adoption. Her age was estimated at 2 years, and she was believed to be a mix of West Highland Terrier and Maltese. She would be available for inspection the next weekend at a local mall.

As I read Pixie's rap sheet and looked at the pictures of her, I weighed the pros and cons of bringing her into our family.

First, she was approximately five years younger than Sully, and I'd had in mind an older female companion for him, one that would take him in tow and teach him to obey simple commands, like "Get the hell away from my fries," and "Stop crapping on my house slippers." At her young age, I wasn't sure Pixie was up to the job.

On the "pro" side of the ledger, she was adorable, and was composed of two of the fifty or so breeds on my Bucket List of dogs I hoped to own before I croaked. And she *did* share a common background with Sully, in that she'd been attacked and injured by a larger dog.

Maybe their mutual experience would give them something to discuss instead of chewing up the upholstery while we were out shopping for groceries.

Despite the overwhelming number of "pros," I still had a few reservations about adopting another dog so soon after losing Ben. What if she didn't have Ben's sweet, loving temperament and his goofy obsession with toys that we found so hilarious? What if Sully hated her and refused to bond with her?

What if I waited until tomorrow before I called the rescue organization, and she'd been adopted by someone else? I ditched my doubts and made the call.

The next weekend we made the hour and a half drive, then sat in the car with Sully for another hour waiting for the mall to open.

I'd contacted the rescue people and expressed interest in Pixie, then filled out their lengthy online questionnaire to see if we were qualified to adopt her, giving as references the rescue organization from which we'd adopted Cheekly and Sully.

We were deemed acceptable adoptive parents, and the woman on the phone advised me to get there early. We would have first dibs on Pixie - *if* we decided to take her. As soon as I saw a guy with keys approaching the doors to the mall, I jumped out of the car and rushed forward. My old man stayed behind to keep Sully company.

In an empty store at the center of the mall, the rescue organization had set up shop with fenced enclosures for the dog adoptees.

Homeless kittehs were housed on blankets inside wire cages for public viewing, and a curtained room at the end of the store allowed interested parties to meet with potential adoptees up close and personal.

Eight small dogs were mixing it up in one of the fenced canine arenas, including two tiny Schnauzers that caught my attention and caused me to go temporarily insane. Their faces looked a lot like Sully's (he was part Schnauzer), and I couldn't resist mauling them a little. They were bonded sisters, though, and needed to be adopted together, and I reluctantly tore myself away.

I scanned the store, looking for Pixie. She wasn't among the pups in the fenced enclosure, and I started to worry that a youthful imposter had impersonated me and had adopted her before I'd walked through the door.

Then my eyes rested on a plumpish, middle-aged woman sitting on a folding chair at the very back of the store. She was clutching a white, tousle-haired pup to her chest and glancing nervously at the crowd that had gathered to inspect the adoptees.

The pup was definitely Pixie, and I guessed the woman holding her was the foster mom who'd been caring for her. I was about to go over to where she was sitting, when a tall, stern-looking woman walked up to me. It was Andrea, head honcho of the rescue group, and the person I'd spoken to on the phone.

"I'm glad you got here early," she told me. "We've had a bit of a problem with Pixie's foster mom, Terry. She's balking about giving Pixie up. But if you decide to adopt her, she'll have no choice in the matter." I glanced back at the woman holding Pixie. She appeared to be in great distress.

"Can I talk to her a minute?" I asked. "She really looks upset."

"Sure, be my guest," Andrea replied. "She's only fostered Pixie for six weeks, but she's become very attached to her. Be warned: she's a little nutty."

I walked back to where Terry was sitting and introduced myself. Her eyes were red and it was obvious she'd been crying. After a few minutes of exchanging sniffled pleasantries, she relaxed her death grip on Pixie and let me hold her.

Dabbing at her eyes with a tissue, Terry explained how the previous she and her husband, Don, had lost two dogs in quick succession, one a Chihuahua and the other a West Highland terrier.

"I was so depressed, I just wanted to die," she confessed. "About the same time my old back injury flared up, and I was in bed for two solid months. My husband was afraid to leave me alone for fear I'd OD on pain meds."

I stroked Pixie's silky head and nodded in sympathy. Terry's story sounded all too familiar to the nightmare I'd been living since Ben's death.

"When I got better and could get around again, I volunteered to foster for the rescue group here. Pixie is my first foster, and I just love this little girl. She reminds me so much of our Westie, Skye…" Terry's voice trailed off. Pixie had put her paws on my shoulders and was giving my face a good cleaning.

"She really likes you," Terry noted. "So far she's been pretty stand offish with strangers, I think because of all the vet procedures she's been through. Anyways, I'd really like to adopt Pixie myself, but my husband says it's way too soon for us to get another dog."

I told Terry our story, how we'd lost two of our dogs in 2013, how we'd adopted Sully for Ben, and how Sully had ended up rescuing all three of us.

Then I told her about Ben's recent death and how sad and lonely Sully was without him - how sad and lonely we *all* were without him. I told her that I thought Pixie would fit perfectly in our "pack," but that I'd understand if she just couldn't bear to part with her.

Terry looked down at the wad of damp Kleenex in her hand, and then at Pixie, who was now sprawled in my lap, napping.

"Nope," she said. "I can see this was meant to be. She's already acting like she's your dog, and I know you'll give her a great home. And I think maybe Don's right about it being too soon for us to get another one."

We both got up and walked back to where Andrea was sitting at her desk, waiting to see who the adoptive parent was going to be. Terry held Pixie while I finished filling out the adoption contract and paid the $200 fee.

Andrea presented me with a goody bag with copies of the adoption contract and Pixie's veterinary records, two cans of dog food, a roll of poop bags, and a few toys that had been donated by rescue sponsors.

"Now, if this adoption doesn't work out, or if your other dog doesn't get along with Pixie, bring her back to us, no questions asked," she said, looking over the rims of her glasses.

"Don't hold your breath," I responded, taking Pixie from Terry, who was sobbing again.

With Pixie's lanky body dangling from one arm, and the goody bag and my purse in the other, I made my way to the front of the store, pausing to turn around and wave goodbye to Terry. But she had already hopped inside the puppy fence and was cuddling the Schnauzer sisters.

Several groups of crazy cat ladies were clustered around the steel cages, oohing and ahhing over the cats and kittens, and jostling each other to see who'd get first pick of the litter.

It was kind of sad to watch them cluck and coo at every Calico and Tabby, and I pitied them for being so thoroughly enslaved by their obsession with cats. The poor souls barely had time for lives of their own.

AUTHOR'S NOTE: A few weeks after we adopted Pixie, Andrea called to see how she was adjusting to her new home. During our conversation I asked her about Terry. "Oh, my God- you won't believe this, but she adopted the two little Schnauzers, and now she's fostering a pregnant Chihuahua-Yorki mix! She says she's probably going to adopt the mother after she's weaned the puppies."

Andrea was wrong. <u>Of course</u> I believed it. Crazy old cat ladies don't have nothin' on crazy old dog ladies, and Terry was about as dog-crazy as they come.

THE MORAL OF THE STORY

"Judge not less ye be judged" – Lonnie May, 1:1

10 - BOO WHO?

My old man and Sully were waiting when I completed the adoption and came back to the car with Pixie. I attached a spare leash to her collar and walked her for a bit in a field next to the parking lot. It was clear she wasn't used to a leash. She pulled and tugged and sniffed at the grass, and didn't do business of any kind.

Terry had given me tips about her, saying that she seemed to be able to hold her pee forever, but that she'd act noticeably nervous if she needed to "go Number 2 potty" as Terry discreetly called it.

When I asked for clarification, Terry leaned over and whispered "You know… if she starts circling around and sniffing her own asshole and what-not."

Pixie wasn't doing either of those things, so I walked her back to the car and put her in the back, about two feet from where Sully was stretched out. He completely ignored her, and neither of them would even look at each other.

As we drove along the highway, the silence in the back seat was deafening. I had NEVER known Sully to be so quiet in the car. Even after a double dose of herbal calming pills, he'd pant and whine and make squeaky noises to alert us to his discomfort.

Unable to contain my curiosity any longer, I turned around to see for myself what was going on. The two were sitting squarely side by side.

Apparently, both had moved toward the center, and now they were practically leaning against each other. They were still looking straight ahead, though, in denial of the presence of another dog. They continued to sit like two stone statues all the way home.

Back at Oceanview, I carried Pixie into the trailer and set her down. She went to Sully's water bowl and drank most of it, then walked over, squatted and pissed an enormous puddle in the middle of the floor.

I got out the Resolve and paper towels, and while I was cleaning up the pee, I noticed her crouching in front of the door, taking a huge Number 2 potty.

In the confusion of her introduction to her new surroundings, she had clearly forgotten to signal us by circling and sniffing her own asshole and what-not.

Sully kept a respectful distance from Pixie that evening, sitting at the opposite end of the sofa from her. When I fed them, she finished first. When Sully was done eating, she moved over to his dish and gave it a second tongue-lapping, and he did the same to hers.

Afterwards they hopped back on the sofa and took up their positions at opposite ends. That night they both slept on our bed, Sully burrowing down to the foot as usual, and Pixie pressing her long, silky-haired (and uncomfortably warm) body against my back.

The next morning we were awakened to growling and snarling noises coming from the living room, and we leapt out of bed prepared to separate two jealous canine combatants.

Instead, we were treated to Sully, lying flat on his back while Pixie stood over him intermittently chewing on his ears and then on his neck. When she paused in her chewing attack, Sully kicked at her with his hind feet to get her started again.

The mock-fighting continued most of the morning until they were both exhausted, at which time they fell asleep snuggled tightly against each other at the same end of the couch. The bond had been forged. From that day on, Pixie and Sully were inseparable.

It was clear that Pixie adored Sully. She followed him everywhere, and when she saw him come to me for his nightly tooth-brushing, she stood beside him, waiting her turn.

My first several attempts weren't entirely successful (Pixie entrapped my hand and the toothbrush with her front paws and tried to push them away), but after a few days she began jockeying to have her teeth brushed *before* I brushed Sully's.

Dog "fight" morning 1
Note shaved area on Pixie's chest

Post dog "fight"

She was a handful on the leash and needed training, but she never tried to run away from us even though she refused to come when we called her.

It eventually occurred to me that the reason she wasn't responding might be because "Pixie" wasn't her real name, and was just the one assigned to her by the rescue people. We'd experienced the same phenomenon with Sully, who'd come to us as "Pepe."

Neither of us cared for that name, least of all, "Pepe." Because of his goofy under bite and round, spikey head, he reminded us of "Sully," the character played by John Goodman in *Monsters, Inc.* Thus, he was re-christened "Sully." He took to it immediately, and everyone was satisfied.

I started trying out different names on her, including names of our previous girl dogs, but none of them suited her and she still wasn't responding when called.

On a whim one day, I tried "Boo," which was the name of the human child the loveable monster Sully took a shine to in the movie. Pixie, who'd been sitting across the room and preoccupied with exploring her nether regions, sprang up and trotted over to me, wagging her tail.

I tried it again later with the same results. Whatever her name was in her former life, I suspected "Boo" sounded something like it. And seeing as how she was white and fluttery, and might look a little like a ghost to some, perhaps Boo *had* been her real name. Whatever the case, she came when we called her "Boo," and it was a giant step forward.

Another piece of information Terry had given me was that she'd never heard Boo bark. She thought perhaps the little dog was incapable of it. And it seemed to be true.

Even when Sully screeched at the sound of a leaf falling on the roof of the trailer, Boo remained silent on the sidelines, listening to his ruckus without comment. It was nothing short of a miracle. Never in our marital history had we owned a dog that didn't bark its brains out, with or without provocation from a falling leaf.

Boo's silence was a first, and a welcome one indeed. We could hardly believe our good fortune, when one afternoon the UPS guy knocked on the door while she was sound asleep on the couch. She shot straight up in the air with a piercing shriek that scared me so bad I had to change my underwear for the second time that day.

The storm of barks and milk-curdling shrieks that issued from her must have had the same effect on the UPS guy, because he dropped the package and ran like hell back to his truck. Our salad days had come to an abrupt end. Boo out-barked any dog we'd ever had, and even Sully had to leave the room when he could stand no more of her marathon screech fits.

Boo is very well-behaved in the car, which is something I couldn't say about Sully until she came along. Her calmness has rubbed off on him a little. She still hasn't entirely adjusted to being on-leash, and she ambles along, dodging right and left until something attracts her interest and she has to investigate.

A few weeks ago we made a weekend trip down the coast to a seaside town with an attraction we'd wanted to see to see for a long time. We took the kids to a local park and began walking one of its many trails.

Everyone was having a pretty cool time of it until Boo suddenly lunged off the trail and into the bushes. I yanked her out by her harness and saw right away that she had a big wad of *something* in her mouth. I don't know why, but I thought it was either paper toweling or a slab of white cake, but whatever it was, I didn't want her to swallow it.

I grabbed Boo's head, forced her jaws open and reached into her mouth. My hand closed around a spongy, disgusting object, and white gooey stuff oozed through my fingers.

It was mayonnaise. The white "wad" was bread from a discarded sandwich. There was no meat visible, and either an animal had disposed of it, or the shithead who chucked the sandwich had eaten the meat and thrown the rest in the bushes.

Out of the 50 million bushes on one of 20 trails within the park, our Boo had managed to find a sandwich. I hadn't felt that sick and repulsed since November 8, 2016.

We turned back down the trail and located a restroom where I tried to drown myself in hand sanitizer. Boo, pissed off at having been denied a second lunch, pouted all the way back to the motel. It took a massage and several Pork Chomp chews to get her back on my side, and it took me a change of clothes and a 20-minute shower to feel properly disinfected.

Over the years, quite a number of assholes have complained that me and my old man treat our dogs like they're our children, and that we spoil and pamper them far beyond the bounds of normalcy. To those folks I can only say:

Shut the hell up, and keep your bratty human kids out of my yard. Go fuck yourself, and then knit a T shirt and imprint "I went and fucked myself and all I got was this lousy T-shirt" on the front of it. I don't have to put up with any more of your nonsense and your stupid opinions.

The fact that you've got nothing better to do than grouse about people and their dogs is pathetic, and I have nothing but scorn for you. If you had dogs to take care of instead of sitting there all day calling people names, fat-shaming women, and tweeting about some meaningless shit, maybe you wouldn't be so obnoxious.

Anyways, as I was saying in this chapter, Boo is the perfect addition to our family. She's everything we could have asked for, and more. We still miss Ben, just not every minute of every day the way we did for a couple months after he died. Boo, like all rescues, is doing her job, and doing it very well.

THE MORAL OF THIS STORY

If you need a *true* friend who will never let you down, and who will love you unconditionally until the day one or the other of you dies, get a dog. And for god's sake, *make it a rescue.*

Sully's new BFF

Boo's first bath

As I was saying, my humans were very easy to train

Somehow, we always manage to get the cutest ones

11 - GEEZERVILLE, USA

After we adopted Boo and had recovered somewhat from the horror of losing Ben, we went back to planning improvements for the yard and trailer.

The 8' X 12' shed we'd ordered was finally delivered, and my old man, tired of trying to work in the confines of the tiny travel trailer, started putting it together. It took several weekends to complete.

After his man cave shed was up and wired, and equipped with fluorescent lighting, we moved his desk, chair and files into it, and painted the outside a nice taupe color.

My old man was extremely happy with his new work space, and indeed, it was almost as elegant as a penthouse office at Trump Tower, only with fewer Russians living next door.

We then set our sights on creating a utility room/half-bath out of the 9' X 12' ramada the previous owner of the lot had used as a carport.

My old man's cave shed
(Ben's grave is on the right, under the tree)

First, my old man put in joists for a raised floor, and then began framing in the walls, leaving openings for a window and door. He wired and plumbed the structure, and I helped him nail on the siding. We installed fluorescent lighting, a standard flush toilet, a laundry sink and a washer and dryer.

At Habitat for Humanity we bought still-in-the-box cabinetry to store cleaning supplies and laundry detergents. After gluing down vinyl floor tiles, we had ourselves a snug little utility room where I could do a load of clothes on-site, and where my old man could sit on the crapper for hours with nothing but a smile and a dog-eared car magazine.

The next project we tackled was building a raised, covered patio and a new boardwalk to replace rotted wood planks that had provided a perilous path to the now-demolished garden shed and to the ramada-turned-laundry shed.

This would turn out to be the most complicated of all of our planned improvements and the one that took the most time. Fortunately, after doing most of the grunt work ourselves when building our last three houses, we had a fairly good idea of the time and effort involved.

Boardwalk
(Laundry shed at back on right)

My old man did all of the measuring and calculations, demolition and disposal of the rotted boardwalk, the transport and placement of concrete footings, the ordering of the lumber, the stacking of the lumber, the sawing of the lumber, the nailing of the lumber, the ordering of the roof panels, the stacking of the roof panels, the dangling from the ladder while installing the roof panels, and the creation of railings with lattice sides so Boo and Sully would have a safe place to play.

Landscaping around deck and boardwalk

I did my part by scanning dozens of samples to find the perfect color for him to use when he stained the wooden structure. I also stood by to steady the ladder while he nailed stuff high up off the ground.

I can honestly say that if we had it all to do over again, I'd probably stay at a motel during the process, as the sawing and hammering and what-have-you were extremely disturbing when I was trying to nap in the afternoon.

By the time we were finished with the indoor and outdoor projects, I was utterly exhausted. I *did* find gratification in the number of geezers who stopped their cars in the middle of the street to admire our work, and to offer their personalized advice for irregularity, toe nail fungus, denture odor and the like.

As more and more geezers returned to Oceanview from their winter homes in the desert, the number of drive-by health consultations increased dramatically, and was expanded to include budgetary advice about where my old man could find the best prices on gel shoe inserts, adult diapers, hearing aids and pharmaceutical concoctions said to promote the regrowth of hair, or restore male vitality.

I faithfully recorded every tip and suggestion the geezers made – not because of any interest on my own part - but in case I needed first aid information for my old man, who, ever since he'd finished building the deck and boardwalks, had been endlessly whining about knee and back pain to a degree I found annoying and cringe-worthy.

One evening he'd even had the nerve to ask me to massage his lower back. Knowing what *that* would lead to, I refused. I was sick and tired of being a trophy wife, a plaything, an upscale distraction for when he wasn't building a shed or staining a deck.

At any rate, I was willing to try almost any cure or possible remedy the Oceanview geezers came up with to avoid having to perform what amounted to a lap dance on a geriatric patient.

Another reason I recorded the musings of our geezerly neighbors was the tremendous popularity of chapters in *Trailer Dogs* 1 and 2 that dealt with the so-called "boomer" generation, and understanding their appalling manners, their ghastly habits, and their shockingly bad behavior in the checkout line at Walmart.

Thousands, if not millions of *Trailer Dogs* fans had contacted me to ask if, in *Trailer Dogs* 3, I'd include more observations about geezers and how to cope with their unpredictability and their tendency to bore the living hell out of everybody with long-winded ramblings, going on and on and on about their ailments, their food preferences, their cats, their snoopy neighbors, their religious beliefs, their politics, the weather, *Everybody Loves Raymond* re-runs, their doctor's snotty receptionist, the 10 pairs of glasses they misplaced last week, the bilious effects raw onions have on their digestive systems, and how they can never find anything on their goddamn computer, including the goddamn on-off switch.

Anyways, I pride myself on giving my reading audience what it wants, and a few things it *doesn't* want, just to keep it on its fungus-ravaged hammer toes.

My experience dealing with a frail, demented old man has given me much insight to the elderly, and now that I am living among so many of them, I felt the need to share my knowledge and expertise.

So, without further delay, I now give you: **GEEZERVILLE, USA**.

Later on in this third volume of *Trailer Dogs*, and again, by popular demand from my followers, I'll also publish many new recipes for you to try out in your trailers, my latest difficulties with Walmart, trailer décor, and, of course, other subjects I can't recall at the moment, and which are probably in my draft Table of Contents, which I am unable to find due to the fucking computer always storing my files under some weird name that I can't remember.

Let's be honest here, folks…you're going to be lucky if I finish writing this book at all, thanks to the computer problems I've been having, along with some gastrointestinal issues that have plagued me ever since I ate a sample roll thingie a Japanese guy, who was dressed like a chef, handed me at Safeway.

It tasted like it had *raw fish* in it. I (involuntarily) spit it out on the floor. The dude tried to poison me, and then he turned around and stared at me *like it was my fault*. So, anyhow, let's get this show on the road.

Why Geezers are Pissed Off All the Time

1. Many geezers are perpetually honked off because something's always hurting.

Like their feet, or their knees, or their bowels, or their teeth, or their sinuses. It helps to relieve the stress caused by these ailments if Geezers can talk about them *at length* to young people to warn them about what's going to happen when *they're* geezers and *their* fucking sinuses are killing them, and they can't even buy the original Advil Cold & Sinus over the counter anymore because some shitwit thinks they'll take it home and make meth out of it. If they wanted meth, why wouldn't they just go over to their neighbors' trailer and buy it straight up?

What the geezers end up doing is taking double doses of some generic meth knock-off that dries up their sinuses like two chunks of petrified wood, and their fucking cheeks pound so hard, they feel like they could kick a sewer rat to death. But see, they can't do that because their goddamn knees are stiff and hurting too bad from sitting around all day, tweeting. (At least this is what I was told by an angry, pissed-off geezer with sinus issues and clunky knees.)

2. Geezers get angry and defensive because they know young people make fun of them behind their backs.

It happens all the time. Pimply-ass young people make degrading, ageist comments about poor doddering old fools who block the aisles at Walmart while they rummage through 3-dollar DVDs looking for the latest Sylvester Stallone movie.

The young smart asses don't realize (and probably don't care) that most old folks wear state-of-the-art hearing devices capable of detecting a hummingbird's fart from 500 yards away.

They also don't appreciate that the humiliated oldsters often seek revenge by clearing phlegm from their nasal passages and directing it toward the row of Skittle bags on the candy aisle, or perhaps in the direction of the handlebars on bicycles parked willy-nilly in front of the store.

One outrageous display of youthful mockery aimed at geezers occurred when Kim Jong Un, the 33-year-old leader of North Korea referred to the President of the United States as "The Dotard."

The unprecedented slur by the leader of a foreign nation barely raised eyebrows, having been outdone by a remark from US Secretary of State Rex Tillerson, a man much closer to the president's own age, when he called Trump a "fucking moron" in front of witnesses.

Joining forces with their youthful counterparts, others in Trump's age group have reportedly referred to him as "an idiot," "a dunce," "the stupidest man I've ever met," "a brain-dead asshole," "a shit-eating, dick-yanking, bonehead," and "a piss-loving, fat crank with delusions of grandeur and barely enough cash to pay off a backstreet hooker with bad teeth."

Although the insults are vulgar and perhaps uncalled for, they are welcome proof that America's First Amendment rights, or our duty to "call 'em as we sees 'em," prevails.

In conclusion, we have all witnessed, on a daily basis, how angry a half-witted, sputtering old moron reacts when young, intelligent people, or even partly sane folks his own age mock him. Two Words: Twitter Rage.

3. Geezers get frustrated because everything they do takes forfuckingever.

I have been told by numerous old people that there are never enough hours in the day when you're living the life of a geezer. It starts in the morning as soon as they drag their asses out of bed and hit the john for the eleventh time since they hit the sack the night before.

Replacing a roll of toilet paper can become an all-day chore when they've forgotten to buy a 12-pack of generic at Walmart, and even if they *had* remembered they were about to run out, they probably forgot to bring their goddamn coupon.

Then there's the obligatory look in the mirror to see what damage has been done overnight, and whether it can be repaired or even temporarily covered up with giant sunglasses and a broad brimmed hat with an attached black veil.

Nothing can be done about their red and swollen eyelids, for blepharitis is incurable among the elderfolk. Follicle-dwelling mites that feed on dead skin cells and cause eyelashes and eyebrows to fall out *will* take their toll.

On the bright side, the microscopic scourge significantly reduces the need for expensive eye makeup, and which, to the fucking mites is like an invitation to dine at a 3-star restaurant.

After cleansing her eyelids and surrounding tissue with exorbitantly priced tea tree oil-laced potions, the female geezer begins the long search for her eyeglasses, which, as we all know, she has shoved to the top of her head in order to avoid slopping tree tea oil on the lenses.

Thirty minutes later, when the eyeglasses have finally been located, they must be rinsed in tepid water to remove the last traces of tea tree oil that the elderbeast accidentally smeared on the lenses as she grappled with them on top of her head.

Author's Note: I interviewed only female geezers for this chapter, as my old man does not allow me to meet with male geezers alone, for lunch, or anything else that might result in him not also receiving a free lunch.

Once her glasses are back in place, The Sheezer, or female geezer, usually repairs to the kitchen area of her trailer (if that's what she happens to live in) to prepare breakfast, - one for herself and one for her two dogs (if she happens to have two dogs), who have already enjoyed their own breakfast and that of The Sheezer's old man.

Regardless of the fact they have already been fed, the dogs seem ravenous, and they jump and scratch relentlessly at The Sheezer's legs, leaving long red claw marks in their wake.

The Sheezer usually drops the dogs' vitamins and calming pills on the floor, and while they are otherwise occupied chasing after them, she turns to the cupboard where the household cereals are kept. She realizes, with some anguish, that the Cheerios box is nearly empty, its contents having been used as treats the day before, when her bastard dogs ran short of Pork Chomps.

As she pours the last of the Cheerios into the bowl, the dogs recommence jumping and clawing at her bare legs, and she makes a mental note to have them both put to sleep sometime in the next few days. It is a mental note forgotten later in the day when she watches them napping together on the couch, looking like two little angels.

After her cereal has been consumed (mostly by the greedy, obnoxious dogs), The Sheezer retires to the bathroom, and, after a long and unfruitful sojourn, makes another mental note to purchase a box of All-Bran, and to email her sister and her friends with all of details of her unexpected bout of constipation.

As with the putting down of the dogs, The Sheezer forgets about buying the All-Bran, but manages to inform each and every recipient in her contact list, including her senators and congressmen, of her constipation diagnosis.

The Sheezer, having completed the most essential of her morning ablutions, then tackles the Brushing of the Teeth, which requires her to fire up the Oral-B electric toothbrush and its various attachments.

When the brushing is done, The Sheezer fills her Waterpik with warm water and turns it on, forgetting to put the nozzle in her mouth first, and flooding the walls and floors with mouthwash-laced tap water.

She regroups, and begins to flush last night's culinary excesses from her gums. She is mildly alarmed at a purple orb dislodged from between her back molars. She does not know what it is.

It could be a blueberry from a fried pie, but she ate that pie last week, and the object will remain unidentified unless it stops up the drain and has to be fished out by The Heezer.

When these tasks are accomplished, The Sheezer reaches for her medications, which consist of approximately 15 boxes of allergy and sinus capsules, none of which does the job like those old boxes of Advil Cold & Sinus did in the days before elder abuse became fashionable and drove the medication from the marketplace.

The Sheezer extracts a blister packet from a box, and begins the thankless and impossible job of tearing off the tiny corner tab that will (supposedly) expose a thin aluminum seal that can be punctured with a thumbnail, revealing the lifesaving capsules. **THIS WILL NOT HAPPEN**.

The corner tab will inevitably break off, waft through the air like a tiny silver glider, and land effortlessly **BEHIND THE FUCKING TOILET**, where it will repose with its brother and sister corner tabs until time immemorial.

The Sheezer will then have no choice other than to attack the bubble pack with a pair of sharp scissors, stabbing and hacking her way through the flimsy aluminum membrane to get at the now-pierced capsules, which have leaked their contents into the tiny aluminum inner chamber.

Mindless of the health risks, she will place the leaky coffin into her mouth and suck its precious cargo down the hatch without benefit of water. It is a morning ritual that will be repeated the next day, and the day after that, until The Sheezer's sinuses finally unclog or she fatally injures herself getting the fucking blister pack open.

Once she has self-medicated, and assuming she's still breathing, The Sheezer will return to the kitchen area to procure coffee, only to find the goddamn machine has turned itself off and the coffee is cold.

While she ponders whether to use her walkie-talkie to summon The Heezer - who is out doing whatever in his fucking shed - of the coffee emergency unfolding inside the trailer, the two dogs start jumping and ripping at The Sheezer's legs again, reopening the wounds they inflicted minutes earlier while demanding breakfast.

"What is their fucking problem?" The Sheezer might wonder aloud. It is then she notices the clock over the refrigerator. It is well past noon, some five hours since she shared the last of her Cheerios with the little shits, and now they are hungry again.

It has taken The Sheezer *that long* to perform simple morning ablutions and properly medicate herself for the day ahead. As she opens a can of dog food, she makes a mental note to have both of them put to sleep sometime in the next few days.

4. Geezers are furious most of the time because they forget stuff and have to go back to the store twenty times before they remember

what they were there for. Sometimes they even forget they were at the store.

I had quite a lot of notes on this particular point, but unfortunately, my old man seems to have misplaced them. I will look for them as soon as I locate my reading glasses.

Now that I've found my glasses and calmed down some, I realize that I don't really need the notes I took while interviewing the angry and forgetful geezer, whom, I finally recalled, was none other than **MY OLD MAN**.

One thing I'll say for myself is that I've got one of the best memories, and that I've probably forgotten more about weed strains than most folks, including old what's-his-name - the pot-smoking geezer who sang *Sad Eyes Are Cryin' in the Rain*, will ever know.

Anyways, my old man just got back from the store.

From a reusable shopping bag, he pulled out a fresh box of wine (to replace the full one that is on the counter), a bag of salt & vinegar kettle chips (which I despise and he loves), his annual purchase of gel body wash, and a plastic sack of blueberry bagels, the smell of which nauseates me so much when they're in the toaster, I have to wait until he's eaten breakfast and gone out to his work shed before I can even get out of bed.

He'd forgotten to pick up his Crestor prescription at the pharmacy, so he had to go back to the store.

This time he came back with another box of wine, more bagels, and still no Crestor. He was trembling with fury because he could think of no good reason to blame Microsoft for his forgetfulness.

The third time was charm, as they say, because on that trip he managed to get the Crestor, along with another box of wine and more of the fucking blueberry bagels.

Even though I am barely half my old man's age and have an aforementioned (somewhere in this magazine) excellent memory, I admit to being *mildly* forgetful at times.

Sometimes I forget the car window's down when I am commenting rather loudly and humorously on the looks, size, species, or dress of someone in the parking lot at Walmart. Thankfully, most of them are slow-moving geezers, so I have been spared many a cane lashing by the walking almost-dead.

5. *Geezers become enraged when they can't get stuff open.*

Some of my younger readers, contemplating this point, are chuckling to themselves, and here's why:

They know, that I know, that they know that I've already partly covered this geezer provocation in my description of The Sheezer, trying in vain to open her sinus medication. The reason for their chuckling is because, like me, they're thinking of all the geezer readers who already forgot I wrote about that. Christ, some people just can't be saved, can they?

Anyways, those blister packs should be outlawed, in my humble opinion. A Sheezer could easily slice up a finger and bleed out before she hit the button on her Medical Alert necklace, which she probably forgot to put on that morning. If it isn't one thing, it's afuckingnother.

Everything in Geezer World is encased in child-proof packaging that only a child with a sound, unclouded mind and strong little fingers can open. Take the shredded cheese that comes in a "resealable" bag.

For one thing, a geezer can't get the bag open without a pair of scissors or a saw blade, and number two, it's only after she's forced to cut the top off that she realizes the "sealable" part got cut off too.

So then there's nothing left to do but sit on the floor and eat the shredded cheese with her fingers. All that cheese isn't good for the geezer heart, which is probably about to explode anyway because of the stress she felt from opening that lousy bag. Today's shredded cheese packaging is abusive to geezers, plain and simple.

Another packaging nightmare for geezers is those tiny bouillon cubes wrapped up in tinfoil like a birthday present for a rat. The ends are folded into microscopic triangles and stuck to the sides of the cube with epoxy.

Geezers, with their stubby arthritic fingers, failing eyesight and short tempers, can't be expected to unwrap one of those goddamn cubes in less than twenty minutes. A lot of times it takes a trip to the toolshed for a hammer and chisel to get the cube de-foiled.

Geezers who still possess a thimbleful of sanity often just skip the whole bouillon cubes ordeal and buy ready-made broth in a can. I can't in good conscience recommend this solution, however, due to the atrocious design of can openers in general, which are commonly known as "Satan's Tool" among mechanically-challenged geezers and left-handed youngsters alike.

Perhaps the most anger-producing product ever to torment the geezer crowd, however, is the corkscrew. This demonic invention has caused more strokes than any other device known to mankind, even the ignominious can opener.

Accurately named, the corkscrew righteously screws up the cork, blocking easy access to what many dispirited geezers call "suicide prevention in a bottle." Rarely does the corkscrew do more than bore a hole through the unsuspecting cork, ripping its innards to shreds, save for the bottom half, which remains firmly lodged in the neck of the bottle.

After tossing the fucking gadget into the nearest trash can, the enterprising geezer will often seek out an ice pick, with which he or she will stab and poke at the ha' cork until it flops ass-first back into the bottle, sucking a thousand cork fragments along with it. An even worse scenario results when the corkscrew fails entirely and the cork cannot be safely removed from the bottle.

Throwing caution to the wind, the desperate, angry geezer may take risks befitting the Flying Wallendas mounting the high wire in 10-inch stilettos.

With few other available options, geezers have been known to carry an uncooperative wine bottle outside, break its neck on the corner of a brick house, and gulp down the contents, heedless of the danger.

I have seen this act of gross geezer stupidity with my own two eyes, and one time I even helped tweeze glass shards out of the foolish geezer's lips and beard.

6. Geezers are furious most of the time because they forget stuff and have to go back to the store twenty times before they remember what they were there for. Sometimes they even forget they were there at all.

As I explained somewhere else in this DVD, my old man misplaced my notes for this chapter, and couldn't remember where he'd put them. After locating my reading glasses, I found the notes in, of all places, the top drawer of my desk.

The thrust of the notes dealt with my old man's terrible memory. Granted, he's worlds older than I am, and his memory has been awful since high school when he forgot to do my math homework.

It's gotten a lot worse, to the point that I have to remind him every day or so, *in detail*, of all the dumb shit he's pulled over the years. I interpret his silence as either gratitude for the life lessons I am teaching him, or the fact that he doesn't hear worth a shit. Whatever the case, the lessons often take hours and many thoughtful pulls on the wine box spigot to impart.

His deteriorating memory recently caused quite a stir in our marital harmony. We were at the bank transferring funds, and the young woman behind the desk (Michelle was her name, as I recall) requested my driver's license for purposes of identification.

The license was from out of state, of course. My old man had already gotten his new license months before, and I had ruined several dozen pairs of underwear laughing at his photo ID, which appeared to have been snapped post-mortem.

I handed my license to Michelle, and she gasped ever so slightly as she inspected it. My old man leaned forward, his swinish red eyes gleaming with delight.

"Not a very flattering picture, is it?" he said, the words dripping with sarcasm from his cavernous mouth, with its stained yellow teeth and gargantuan flaccid tongue.

"Oh, it's not that," Michelle answered. "In fact, her picture's *a lot* better than my photo ID. Mine looks like a mug shot!"

I chuckled softly. Indeed, Michelle was not the most attractive flower in the garden. Even though she had to be in her mid-twenties, she already had the pinch-faced, defeated look of a woman who'd been married a couple months. She handed the license back, and with it a piece of advice:

"I noticed your license is going to expire in two weeks. You should apply for a new one right away. If you miss the expiration date, you'll have to take the driving test, and the folks at the DMV are *really* gung-ho."

When we got home, I decided to skip that day's life lessons for my old man, and instead, pump him for information about what to expect at the DMV.

I needed to know whether they would insist on confirming my actual weight on a scale, whether I could ask for a re-take if I didn't like my ID photo, and most importantly, whether there was a written test for which I needed him to give me the correct answers beforehand.

He assured me they would accept whatever weight I wrote down and that there wasn't a written test. As to whether they would allow a re-take of the ID photo, he *did not recaaaaaw.*

On Friday, we showed up at the DMV around 3pm, thinking if it was late enough in the day, the staff would be more likely to rush us on through before closing time at 5.

The room was packed with frustrated-looking individuals, each of whom was holding a small slip of paper with a number on it.

I took a slip from the number machine. It was 52. We sat down just as Number 32 was called. An hour later we were still sitting. Quite a few people had given up and left, and we were about ready to do the same when Number 51 was called. My old man gave the "thumbs up" sign as geezers often do, and we sat back down.

Fifteen minutes after Number 51 had completed his title transfer, my number was called. I grabbed my purse and the manila envelope I'd brought along containing my birth certificate, a utility receipt from Oceanview, and my current license.

At the counter, the woman asked how she could help me, and I told her I was applying for a driver's license. Then I handed her all my info, including an application form I'd filled out while I was waiting.

She seemed extremely pleased that I'd remembered to bring everything with me, and she didn't question the weight I'd written down. Amazingly, it was the same as when I applied for a Beginner's Permit at age 15, and I had lied about it then as well.

"That'll be $5 for the test," she said. "When you're finished, come back to the counter and I'll give you a temporary license to use until yours comes in the mail. If you have any questions or encounter problems while you're taking the test, use the phone next to the computer to call me. "

Wait... what in the hell was this?

"I don't think you understand," I told her. "I'm just *renewing* my license, and I don't need to take a test. I've been driving for years, and I'm very good behind the wheel. No accidents or arrests to speak of."

"There isn't a *road* test," she informed me, "But we have to administer a written test to make sure you're familiar with the laws in this state. Don't worry about it, sweetie. The test is easy-peasy! You can miss 7 questions and still pass."

I thought about this for a minute. I didn't like her demeaning "sweetie" bullshit, but she might be right about the test. I *was* an excellent driver, and my brain was one of the best, at least according to an IQ test I'd taken in *Cosmopolitan Magazine* in 1987. Or was that a career aptitude quiz? And it might have been in *National Lampoon*. I wasn't sure.

Thinking back, it was *definitely* a career aptitude quiz in *Cosmo*, and I had passed it standing on my head, although I chose not to pursue a career as a grave digger. And that was mainly due to discriminatory practices at funeral parlors in those days.

Thinking about the successful IQ test in *Cosmo*, my self-confidence started to build, and I decided to spin the wheel of fortune and take the driver's test.

On my way to the computerized test area, I whacked my old man in the back of his enormous head with the rolled-up envelope and hissed "asshat" in his ear for lying to me about the test requirement.

Several geezers overheard my admonishment and turned in their seats to glare at me accusingly. I ignored them and sat down at the desk.

Nothing was happening on the computer screen, and I was about to pick up the phone to call for help when instructions popped up. They were barely visible in a tiny font, and I had to practically press my nose against the screen to make out what they said.

None of the words made sense, and I couldn't focus. Perspiration rolled down the back of neck. It was possible the test was in another language, maybe French or German. I sucked in a lungful of air and clicked on what appeared to be **PROCEED TO TEST**.

The first question had something to do with a motorcycle. What the hell was this? I was applying for a license to drive a car, not a fucking chopper. I clicked on one of three possible answers, and a big red X appeared next to the question. That couldn't be a good sign.

I picked up the phone to complain about the unfair question, but no one answered. The woman at the counter was busy with another customer, so I cradled the receiver between my neck and chin, and went on to the next question.

It had to do with changing lanes in a "roundabout." *Asfuckingif.* One thing I knew for sure: Roundabouts were in England, not in America. In America we drive on FREEways, where we are FREE to change lanes whenever we damn well please, and without signaling.

I clicked on an answer and another red X appeared. The goddamn phone was still dead as a doornail, so I couldn't call for assistance or to register a complaint.

The test was clearly breaching my Constitutional driving rights, and I made a mental note to report the violation to the ACLU as soon as I got home. I was sweating even more now, my ears were ringing, and I felt that at any moment I was going to blow. I was having disturbing visions of attacking everyone in the room and ripping them to shreds with my bare teeth.

The questions got harder and harder, and it was pretty obvious I'd been given a test intended for a citizen of Great Britain.

The cars in the diagrams were of an odd, boxy styling, and seemed to be traveling on the wrong side of the road, either intentionally or to trick me into answering incorrectly, which I was doing with greater frequency.

When the test ended, "RETURN TO COUNTER" appeared on the screen. It didn't seem encouraging. I got up from the desk, retrieved my purse and walked toward the counter, forgetting to let go of the phone receiver and nearly ripping the cord from the wall. I heard derisive clucks and chuckles coming from the vicinity of the geezer gallery.

"Oh my, I'm so sorry, but you missed one too many of the questions," the woman at the counter informed me woefully. "You'll need to take the test again."

"This is an outrage," I told her, trying my best to control my anger.

"First, my old man gets his license here, and he says you didn't make *him* take a test. Then I come in and wait 5 hours, and you tell me there *is* a test, but it's so easy-friggin'-peasy that I should go ahead and take it, even though I didn't study for it on account of my old man's a damn liar!"

The woman was staring at me incredulously, her mouth hanging open. I delivered the final punch.

"And to top it all off, the test has questions about driving in England on roundabouts and riding motorcycles, and the phone didn't work when I tried to call you to report the atrocities."

"Um… did you see the sign next to the big red button that says *PRESS TO CALL FOR ASSISTANCE*?

I ignored her pathetic attempt at a cover-up.

"All I'm telling you is that the phone didn't work and the questions weren't American. That's all I have to say about it... *for now*."

I let the *'for now'* hang in the air as a warning. No need to tell her that a representative from the ACLU would soon be knocking at her door. She glanced up at the clock. Closing time was fast approaching and she still had an understandably irate customer to deal with.

"I'll tell you what," she said conspiratorially. "If you get here when we open at 9am next Monday, my assistant will be here to help me, and I'll make sure to take you first. You'll have all weekend to study for the test, and I'll keep your forms right here at the desk so you won't have to fill them out again. Now, the bad news is, you'll have to pay another $5 for the re-test."

I considered the offer. It was patently unfair, and probably another violation of my Driving Rights. I didn't think I should have to pay another $5 to take a test about foreign driving rules and regulations.

"Can you guarantee I'll get an American test next time?" I asked. She nodded, probably grateful I wasn't making a Citizen's Arrest.

"You've got my word on it. Anyway, people *never* get the same test twice. Why, they'd know all the correct answers, wouldn't they?"

When we got home I sat my old man down for his Life Lesson. After several hours of enhanced instruction, he finally admitted that he *had* taken a test when he'd applied for his new license, and not only that, he'd *studied the manual for two days beforehand*.

He'd forgotten all about it until just now, and he was heartily sorry for causing me to fail my test and for being such a big fat stupid liar. To make it up to me, he broke open another box of wine, brought Taco Bell home for supper, and gave me a 30 minute massage as a kicker.

That weekend I did nothing other than study for the test, using online practice exams and the manual I'd picked up on the way out of the DMV. By Sunday night I had memorized every answer to every possible question, including the unethical ones about roundabouts and motorcycles.

On Monday morning we were in front of the DMV at a quarter of nine. Several sleepy-looking geezers had beat us there, along with a teenage girl who was rocking back and forth heel-to-toe, nervously anticipating her road test.

When the door was unlocked we all filed in, and the geezers each took a number. I held back, expecting to be the first one served as I had been promised. But the woman behind the counter wasn't the same one who'd been there on Friday and had promised me first dibs. And there was no "helper" to be seen.

I angrily yanked a number out of the machine (a 5) and plopped down in the seat next to my old man. An hour later my number was called.

I strode to the counter and gave the woman my name. I started to recite the facts surrounding the ill treatment I'd received the previous Friday, but she said her partner, who was administering the road test to the teenage girl, had told her all about me, and she'd left my forms - filled out and ready to go.

Even better, they were waiving the $5 re-test fee! I took a seat at the computer, clicked on PROCEED TO TEST, and up popped the first question.

It was about motorcycles. It was the exact same test I'd taken before. I thought about telling the woman at the counter about the error, but I didn't want to cause any more trouble than my old man had caused her already.

A young guy sitting at the computer next to me was clearly having trouble, and I looked at him sympathetically.

He kept muttering "fuck" every time he missed a question. Finally he slammed his fist on the keyboard, said "fuck this shit," got up and walked out the door. It was troubling to see such a foul display of temper and hear such profanity coming from a non-geezer male.

Anyways, I breezed through the test in a matter of minutes and scored 100%. The new gal at the counter beamed with pride at my success as she entered data from my form onto my license application. She directed me to sit in a folding chair against the wall while she snapped my photo.

Back at the counter I forked over $55, and she handed me a folded card to be replaced by a permanent license that would come in the mail in a couple weeks.

She congratulated me, and said she'd see me in about eight years if she was still around. I was ecstatic! I skipped over to where my old man sat, and he was grinning from ear to enormous ear with relief and happiness.

"So, you aced the test and got your license," he congratulated me. "Let's take a look at the prize."

He took the temporary license from me and glanced down at it. A look of disbelief and horror passed over his already horrific face, and he turned a shade of white I'd never seen before on a living human. He slowly handed the card back to me.

The photo ID. It was a hideous monster, worse even than the Shrek-like face plastered on his own ID. But according to information on the license, the "monster" only weighed 125 pounds. So what the fuck did she care?

THE MORAL OF THIS STORY

Always leave plenty of room when passing a motorcycle so if the rider falls, you won't run over his big dumb head. Also: Never show your photo ID to your old man when he's wearing tan pants.

12 - TRAILER BEAUTIFUL

In the olden days, we had a pretty sweet life. We lived far out in the sticks on ten acres, and our nearest neighbor was a quarter-mile away.

Back in those days, we had complete privacy, a fenced back yard, a detached 3-car garage with a workshop, loft and three-quarter bath, and a 2800 square foot ranch house with a big front porch. We built the house ourselves, and planned to live there for the rest of our lives.

Then, in 2013, everything changed because right-wing racists' extreme butt-hurt over the first black president caused them to shut down the government.

Federal contracts were put on hold or cancelled altogether, and our small, self-financed, and until then, thriving business came tumbling down, and we had to start all over again. Fortunately, my old man was in a line of work in high demand, and he was able to find a good paying job, but it was two hours away, in the city.

We reluctantly put our house on the market, sold or gave away most of our belongings and furnishings, and took up residence in a 23-foot travel trailer, which we moved to a trailer park 45 minutes from my old man's office.

After a month of camping inside a toaster oven with two dogs and woefully inadequate air conditioning, we went out and bought a used 29-foot 5th wheel, put the travel trailer in storage, and began trying again to adjust to trailer life with 6 more feet of living space and two hydraulic slide-outs.

A couple years later my old man decided he wanted to retire and devote the rest of his life to aggravating the living shit out of me, and he wanted to do it in the Pacific Northwest where we'd lived years before.

The main reason we'd moved from the PNW in the first place was because neither one of us could take another summer, winter, spring, and fall of gloomy, rainy weather. So, we packed up and moved to the desert southwest, built a house, and immediately commenced complaining about the lack of rain and the intense heat that drove us indoors in the summer, fall, winter and spring.

I'm not one to toot my own horn, but in addition to being incredibly brilliant and rarely wrong about anything (at least that's what people tell me), I have always been somewhat of a savant, particularly in the art of interior decoration.

My hillfolk relatives attest to my talent, and have done so ever since the Christmas I gave them all "Travis the Singing Trout" plaques to hang in their huts and lean-tos.

My dear brother is the only member of my family who thinks otherwise. Of an abstract painting I'd recently purchased, he commented: *"It looks like something a damn first grader went and colored."*

I would have been even more wounded had I not heard him refer to a Monet masterpiece as "Three Broads in a Boat." The artistic gene hidden deep in the recesses of our dubious family tree has entirely passed him by. It's a hereditary thing, and nothing can be done about it.

In our previous life, me and my old man had always lived in houses that offered a reasonable amount of wall space and open areas that could be filled with fine art and chic furniture, had we been able to afford them.

To aid me in my quest for aesthetically pleasing decoration, I had often consulted *House Beautiful*, tearing out pages with appealing designs and color schemes. The furnishings pictured in *HB* were, even back then, way beyond our middle class budget, but they gave me ideas about how to recreate the exquisite tableaus with purchases from Target and Ashley Home Store.

In our new life, however, our impoverished decorating budget forced me to rely mainly on yard sales and St. Vincent de Paul. Despite this challenge, I was determined to create a classy, elegant trailer living space for ourselves and the dogs.

With that in mind, I bought a copy of *House Beautiful* and began thumbing through it. Almost immediately I realized my terrible mistake. I had accidentally picked up the *British* edition of the magazine...

The first hint of my error was on a page where readers commented on various construction and design issues they had faced. *House Beautiful* editors selected a few of the letters, published them, and awarded a prize to the letter they thought was the best. A lucky entrant in the *HB* issue I'd bought had won a set of two pans worth £100. What the hell was up with *that*, I wondered?

Since when had a dollar sign transformed itself into a capital L with a hash mark through the middle? I hadn't bought *HB* in quite a while, and maybe the £ was the editors' way of making the pans seem like they were worth more than a hundred dollars.

But the pans didn't look to me like they'd be worth fifty bucks, let alone a hundred. I'd seen better deals at Walmart priced at $29 for a 10-piece set. (**NOTE TO SELF**: *Consider cheap pans as prize for reader who submits best Trailer Dogs review*.) (**NOTE TO SELF**: *Don't forget to delete the NOTE TO SELF about the "cheap" prize idea.*)

Anyways, I began to notice snobby misspellings in the magazine: fav**ou**rite for favorite, neighb**our** for neighbor, col**our**, for color, fl**our** for flower, organ**ise** for organize, glam**our** for glammer.

The list of affectations went on and on, until I was reminded of postcards I received from a classmate when she went to London for 10 days with her parents. Even though it was the first time she'd ever been out of the country, the postcards were chock full of pretentions like: "Me Mum's twat is on the loo," and "Crikey, if I'm going steady with that bloody-ass, sodder Pete when I return from holiday."

Always a motor mouth and inclined to dominate every conversation, when she got back from "holiday," she went around boring the shit out of people with a fake British accent and newly found high-falutin' profanities. She became so insufferable that Sodder Pete finally dumped her for a girl who didn't complain when he put his jack in her boot.

Probably the weirdest thing I came across in the British *House Beautiful* was a description of some sort of stove, which in England they call a "cooker." The Brits refer to burners on the "cooker" as "hobs," and they boil water in "tea kettles" on the "hobs," and (I guess) heat their frozen burritos in the "cooker."

At least that's what I gathered from the ads. Most Americans would be flabbergasted to learn that British cookers and hobs look *exactly* like our stoves and ovens, and are probably yet another example of a foreign country stealing our technology.

It's possible the hob knobs on the cookers have different symbols on them for high, medium and low heat. I didn't get that far in the ad before I had to go change my underwear after reading the words "cooker" and "hobs."

In that same issue of *HB* they were having a contest to win a cooker. I would have filled out the entry blank, but it required that I correctly answer the question *"How many zones does the induction hob have?"* When my supply of underwear ran out, I gave up entirely. In retrospect, the contest was probably rigged anyway.

After my frightful experience with foreign roundabout questions on my driver's test, followed by my awakening to the unprecedented intrusion of English words into our American vocabulary, I was starting to suspect that the Redcoats were up to no good again.

Having witnessed the success of Russians in our 2016 elections, it seemed likely the Brits were also plotting to regain territories lost to them when they were defeated by us Yanks at Waterloo.

As despicable as their treachery is to me, the elderly British monarch, Queen Elizabeth, with her whacko hats and motherly ta-tas, is far more appealing than the Putin-Trump regime, both in terms of good looks and the old gal's smokin' hot, red-haired grandson, Harry. Better red than dead, as they say.

Anyhow, I *did* glean some excellent decorating advice from the British *House Beautiful* - tips that would serve me well in refurbishing our tiny rolling flat, with its moth-eaten beef curtains and its recliners, which were shedding threads faster than minge on a sheezer. *(See Glossary of British Words at boot of book)*

Indeed, I ordered a jolly good gas cooker straight away, as the hobs in our old cooker weren't lighting properly, and had to be consigned to the rubbish pile.

It was unlikely that I was going to be able to fit any of our large paintings, most of which we'd bought at antique malls or co-op art galleries, in the trailer. I was deeply attached to the pieces and didn't want to part with them, so my old man figured out a way to display them in the utility/bathroom shed.

Having a bowel movement under a beloved Robert Motherwell poster in a laundry shed is an experience that cannot be duplicated no matter what your station in life, even though it will never make the pages of *Architectural Digest*.

Art gallery in a can

To satisfy our thirst for culture (mine, anyway), we suspended a couple of our smaller favorite paintings on thin chains my old man attached to the undersides of cabinets in the living area. We've grown accustomed to them dangling down behind the sofa and recliners, and we only crack our heads on them 3 or 4 times a day now. It is called "suffering for one's art."

The artistic gratification is worth the cuts and bruises, though, and the paintings remind us of our privileged past in America's middle class, when we didn't have to rely on free medical advice from the internet and didn't worry about whether our flat's tyres would go flat.

Trailer beautiful

The artistic gratification is worth the cuts and bruises, though, and the paintings remind us of our privileged past in America's middle class, when we didn't have to rely on free medical advice from the internet and didn't worry about whether our flat's tyres would go flat.

Trailer beautiful

and its recliners, which were shedding threads faster than minge on a sheezer. *(See Glossary of British Words at boot of book)*

Indeed, I ordered a jolly good gas cooker straight away, as the hobs in our old cooker weren't lighting properly, and had to be consigned to the rubbish pile.

It was unlikely that I was going to be able to fit any of our large paintings, most of which we'd bought at antique malls or co-op art galleries, in the trailer. I was deeply attached to the pieces and didn't want to part with them, so my old man figured out a way to display them in the utility/bathroom shed.

Having a bowel movement under a beloved Robert Motherwell poster in a laundry shed is an experience that cannot be duplicated no matter what your station in life, even though it will never make the pages of *Architectural Digest*.

Art gallery in a can

To satisfy our thirst for culture (mine, anyway), we suspended a couple of our smaller favorite paintings on thin chains my old man attached to the undersides of cabinets in the living area. We've grown accustomed to them dangling down behind the sofa and recliners, and we only crack our heads on them 3 or 4 times a day now. It is called "suffering for one's art."

THE MORAL OF THIS STORY

Unless you're married to Ralph Lauren, never let your old man decorate your trailer. And if you *are* married to Ralph Lauren, BEWARE: Most of the shit in his store won't fit in your trailer, and you can't afford it anyway.

Also…

In England, they don't have *trailers*. The Brits call them *caravans*. So, if you ever go over there and get stuck on a "roundabout" looking for the exit to a *trailer park*, you are royally fecked, ya bloody duffer.

One of the first rules of successful interior decoration is to *make the space your own*. Really fucking rich people hire expensive designers to interpret their taste and to travel the world, "curating" furnishings for their homes.

Sometimes this works out; sometimes it produces a gilded shitbox like the Trumps' penthouse apartment in New York. When you live in a trailer, however, taste is often a matter of the availability of quality merchandise you can "curate" from Goodwill or St. Vincent Du Paul.

Fortunately, the geezer bumpkins who live and shop Oceanview's thrift stores don't have my sophistication and refinement, and I am able to re-purchase items I donated just the month before.

Occasionally, my old man complains that his taste is not being fully represented in our new abode, and it was with that in mind that I allowed him to decorate spaces on his own, such as the shelf on his side of the closet, his plastic outdoor tool shed, and, of course, his work/hobby shed.

I have, thus far, been able to keep these spaces locked and closed off to visitors from the local health department.

13 - FIENDS & NEIGHBORS

During our first days at Oceanview, we met only one neighbor, Stan Carlyle, whom I took to calling "Sasquatch Stan" because of his giant fake foot and the unpleasant smell that lingered whenever he was nearby.

We hadn't met Stan's wife. He'd said she suffered with arthritis and stayed inside their trailer most of the time, probably doped up on pain killers. The damp, cold climate at Oceanview was no friend to arthritics, that was for sure.

Stan was frequently visited by an old guy, a scrawny little dude, who'd drive up in a battered pick-up truck plastered with Obama-insulting bumper stickers. On the side of the truck, someone had hand-painted the words "Lock her up!" The owner of the truck was clearly the same chump who'd nearly hit us as were leaving Oceanview the previous year after buying our lot.

I learned later that the guy's name was Zeke, and that he "checked up on" Stan's trailer when Stan and his wife were away. Stan was dismayed at the number of petty thefts Zeke reported while he was gone, which was curiously high, seeing as how Zeke was the only person who ever set foot on the property other than Stan and his wife.

Based on the loud voices and guffawing we heard whenever Zeke visited Stan, I guessed that serious quantities of alcohol were involved.

As the weather got better and better, more residents arrived at Oceanview from their southern habitats. Our neighbors on the corner, whom we hadn't even gotten to know, were only back a week or so when they put their lot and trailer on the market.

It sold within days for a (very high we thought) asking price. Maybe Sasquatch Stan had been right when he'd said property values were on the rise at Oceanview.

Some Oceanview dwellers didn't stay at the park all the time, but came on weekends, or for several weeks at a time to enjoy boating activities, ocean fishing, or just breaks from city life. Weekends could get noisy, and the extra traffic was a nuisance in town, but for the most part we were tucked away in the pines and left alone.

We didn't participate in Oceanview's clubhouse goings-on, mainly because we were too busy fixing up our own place to get roped into volunteering to host potlucks or coordinating park clean-up days.

Anyways, me and my old man have never been "joiners" in group activities. Twice, we've lived next to a golf course despite the fact that neither one of us plays golf, although we do enjoy napping to it when it's on TV.

We built a cabin in a popular ski area, but we didn't use it much because the snow kept us from going outside and possibly getting wet and cold. So we sold it. Our last house was in a community of horse lovers, but we didn't own horses due to our fear they might bite us or trample our dogs to death.

During morning and afternoon dog walks at Oceanview, we tried to introduce ourselves to other couples who were strolling around the park, but the conversations never lasted long because Sully and Boo shrieked at the hapless strangers until they gave up and walked away.

The same went for other dogs, squirrels, and the many cats who made their home at the park. Sully and Boo didn't like any of them, and would bark themselves hoarse any time they saw a perceived enemy.

I was fairly certain many of the people we came in contact with hated Sully and Boo, just because they couldn't control their screech-barking and their clawing and lunging at them. I often saw walkers turn and scurry off in another direction when they saw us coming, even if we didn't have Sully and Boo with us.

And that suited me just fine. Because, by god, if there's one thing I won't put up with, it's people who don't like dogs.

The Boys in the Van

The couple at the site directly behind ours didn't show up until we'd been living at Oceanview for two months. We were leaving the park one afternoon, when a large white van pulled into their driveway.

An average-looking guy wearing an un-tucked plaid shirt got out on the passenger side. We passed by too quickly for me to get a good look at the driver, but I did get a glimpse of a young boy, possibly 6 or 7 years old, when he bounced out of the back of the van and ran up the driveway.

Every fucking day thereafter, one or the other of the couple sat out on their covered deck and smoked.

The smoking started early in the morning and didn't let up until they went to bed. I wouldn't have minded at all had they been toking up on weed, but the smoke wafting over the fence was from cigarettes, probably those stinking Player firesticks Canadians are so fond of. That made me a little concerned that we might be living next door to smoking corn holers.

Anyways, whatever brand they were, the smoke from those tors made me nauseous every time I went outside, when I opened a window, or when I was spying on their activities from the bushes. It didn't seem to be doing much for "Smoky Joe" and his old lady either, because their fits of coughing lasted for an eternity, until one or the other fetched a glass of water.

Another annoying thing about the Smoky Joes was the wife's voice, which was inordinately high-pitched, and her laugh, which was basically a series of loud shrieks followed by an outright, lingering scream that put Boo's outbursts to shame.

She'd sit out on the deck with Smoky Joe, and between the clouds of smoke blowing our way and the screeches, my sphincter muscle would tighten up so much, sometimes I couldn't rise from the lounge chair without pulling the cushion loose.

Added to those irritations was their young son, who had memorized a song about Popeye, which he sang repeatedly while running to and fro on their deck wearing what had to be a pair of wooden clogs.

All day long, musical stylings of "Shiver me timbers, blow me down, if anyone steals me goyle..." filtered through the bushes separating our properties. It escaped me how the kid could take in enough oxygen to keep up the endless serenade in that smoke-filled environment. At times the smoke was so thick, I could smell it even inside the laundry shed, and occasionally, inside the trailer.

On Saturday mornings, the Joes usually slept in, and if I wasn't still sacked out myself, I could get up early enough to do a couple loads of wash or pull up a few weeds, and still avoid the smoke/clomp/shriek/Popeye tune brigade.

One such morning I was squatting at the edge of the yard, yanking dandelions and enjoying the peace and quiet, when an excessively homely, obese man, dressed in baggy shorts, socks with sandals, and wearing a floppy sunhat, came crashing through the bushes right in front of me. I let out a yelp and fell backwards, flat on my ass.

The trespasser, probably fearing he'd brought on an implausible heart attack in such a young woman, was equally alarmed. We stared at each other for a second until my attacker finally found his voice, which was several loud shrieks, followed by a familiar high-octave, lingering scream.

"Oh, dear God," he squealed, failing to stifle another screech. "What have I done? I think I may have gone and killed our beautiful, sexy neighbor!"

He reached out a plump hand and helped me to my feet. Moved by the sincerity of his apology and keen powers of observation, I felt a touch of guilt for having thought him so annoying and homely just a minute before.

We introduced ourselves. His name was Lance, and his husband (the man in the plaid shirt I'd seen getting out of the white van), was Wade. The boy was their adopted son, Matt.

I was taken aback at the realization that we'd been living so close to a gay couple who smoked cheap cigarettes, weren't seriously good-looking, and who dressed worse than my old man.

It just didn't seem possible. When Lance praised the improvements we'd made to our lot as being nothing less than "spectacular," I thanked my lucky stars that were at last living next to people with whom we could undoubtedly establish a close friendship. It stood to reason.

In high school, I had earned the nickname "queer bait" due to the fact that I hung out with a group of gay boys, each of them incredibly witty and delicately handsome, and each of them eschewing sweatshirts and jeans for button-up shirts and neatly pressed slacks.

Back then, as many are to this day, gays were relentlessly teased and bullied by jocks and hoods alike. But unlike members of today's LGBT community, my gay pals tolerated the abuse with an abundance of peaceful forbearance, saving razor-sharp criticisms of their tormentors for our noon gathering in the school's lunch hall. They were my kind of people.

Among the gayest of my gay friends was Scottie Gold. Scottie was a year behind me, but was in my Algebra II math class. (**NOTE TO READERS:** *Algebra II. I know what you're thinking. Shut the hell up.*)

Anyways, every afternoon after we'd take our seats, and before our teacher came in, Mike Drake, the biggest asshole jock in the whole school, would swagger over to Scottie's desk, and without a word, take the pencil from Scottie's hand or from the desk's pencil holder, walk to the window, and toss it out.

Our classroom was on the second floor and there was no chance for Scottie to retrieve the pencil, so he took to buying a new package each week to replace the tossed ones. This mistreatment happened every day without fail, and provided splendid entertainment for the jocks 'n hoods crowd.

On one occasion, Scottie tried to take control of the situation by ceremoniously holding his pencil up for all to see, then walking over to the window and tossing it out himself.

His unanticipated show of cheekiness didn't go over well at all with Drake and his miscreant friends, however. Deprived of the opportunity to humiliate "the queer," Drake got up from his desk and approached Scottie, holding out his giant palm and fixing Scottie with an intimidating stare.

Humiliated, and not wishing to invite further abuse or possible injury, Scottie dutifully obliged, pulling a second pencil from his pack of spares and handing it over to his tormentor. Drake had just enough time before our teacher walked in to toss the second pencil out the window, and return to his seat amid snorts and guffaws from his team of fellow shitheads.

Now, I was not, by a long fucking shot, "Miss Popularity" in high school. Even though I was pretty hot stuff back then, resembling an uglier, porkier version of Princess Diana, I lived on the wrong side of the tracks with a widowed mom who worked as a waitress to support us.

I had neither the expensive clothes and shoes, nor the desire to flatter my way into groups of girls whose only desire in life seemed to be hooking up with ignoramus bozos like Mike Drake.

Furthermore, I was known for being a sharp-tongued put-down artist who took shit from no one, not even teachers.

How I'd gotten this dubious reputation puzzles me to this very day, but that's another subject, and I don't have time to satisfy readers' meddlesome curiosity, as I am in the middle of writing *Trailer Dogs 3*, which you would plainly see if you weren't so busy stuffing your fucking pie holes with chocolate and sucking down Dr. Pepper by the quart.

Anyways, as I was saying, Drake's cruelty toward the better-looking and infinitely more intelligent Scottie didn't sit well with me. If Scottie was too nice to take Drake's ass down, well, let's just say, I *wasn't*. I vowed to myself that one way or another I would get revenge on behalf of my gay friend.

Drake's day of reckoning was a long time coming, as football season was upon us, and he frequently got excused from class to attend practice. We never knew when he'd be in attendance, and some days when he *did* show up, he was too distracted, probably by unseemly thoughts about his vapid cheerleading girlfriend, to bother with bullying Scottie.

One Monday afternoon, my opportunity arose quite by chance when the fire alarm sounded, and students, familiar with the drill, abandoned their text books and sweaters, and began moving toward the door.

Our teacher, Mr. McNeal, an absent-minded geezer at 41 if there ever was one, walked out with the first group of kids, leaving the rest of us behind to fight the imaginary flames on our own. Scottie waited by the door for me to join him in the exodus, but I waved him on and stayed behind in the empty classroom.

After making sure nobody else was around, I went to Drake's desk, gathered up all his text books, his notebook, his zippered envelope of pens and pencils and his jacket, and carried the loot over to the window.

Looking out, I saw my classmates, Scottie and Drake among them, lining up along the edge of the football field. I stood, hidden from view at the side of the window old McNeal had conveniently forgotten to close, and tossed Drake's belongings out one by one.

When the last of his papers had fluttered to the ground, I hastily made my way to the girl's restroom and hid in a stall until I heard the "all clear" bell ring. As students filed back into their classrooms, I integrated myself with the horde, unnoticed.

Obeying the unspoken law of never confessing one's criminal behavior to one's closest friend, lover, or even one's two-bit, fixer lawyer, I didn't tell Scottie I was the one who'd dumped Drake's stuff out the window, although I'm 100% certain he knew it was me.

Amazingly enough, the deed seemed to go unnoticed by my classmates, and Drake maintained his cool as though nothing at all had happened. He remained the school's jock hero, and if or how he ever retrieved his goods is unknown to me, as is whether he continued to throw Scottie's pencils out the window.

I was transferred out of the Algebra II class shortly thereafter and demoted back to remedial Algebra I. Scottie never brought up the subject of the pencil-tossing, and we both wisely avoided the topic.

I hooked up with my future old man about that time and quickly lost interest in hanging with my gay pals, having discovered different "activities" to pursue on weekends. It was a choice forced upon me by hormonal influences over which I had no control, and also by my future old man's mathematical skills, which allowed me to pass Algebra I without doing any homework.

But I digress again.

The gay couple living behind us were also owners of two adorable, long-haired Chihuahuas who yapped and carried on almost as much as Sully and Boo did, adding to the hyena laughter, Popeye ditty, and clomping of 7-year-old boy feet coming from their side of the property line. After he'd apologized again for startling me, Lance said he was sorry if their dogs' barking disturbed us.

"They get very upset when we leave them alone for any length of time, and when we come home they're waiting to punish us with their yips and yaps!" Lance said, emphasizing the humorous tidbit with one of his eardrum-shattering laugh-shrieks.

"Don't think a thing of it," I reassured him. "Our Sully and Boo make enough noise for the whole neighborhood. They bark at *everything*, even when a leaf falls on the deck."

"Yes, well, about your dogs…" Lance began, pausing as if to find exactly the right words. "I wanted to speak to you about *that*. Wade and I are hosting a little soire for some people tomorrow evening, and I super-hate to ask you, but would you mind keeping them inside during the party? Those little guys get awfully noisy with their barking and carrying on. And it's just for one night."

I stood there wondering if I could drive the toe of my plastic Slogger up Lance's ass without toppling over again. There was really no way to do it, not without risking another fall. How *dare* he, after all the smoke and singing and clomping we'd put up with out of him and his family?

And how fucking *dare* he not even think to invite us to their sorry party, which was probably going to just be a gaggle of old queens sitting around, mocking us straight folks over our taste in box wines, and our inability to decorate our homes and trailers using more than one patterned fabric.

The more I thought about it, the more enraged I became at his rudeness, and the strong possibility he had been referring to my old man and not me as their "sexy neighbor."

What had happened to the Scottie Golds of this world, some of whom stayed in the closet so long they could no longer see the crack of light shining through from the other side of the door?

Had all of them jumped ship and joined the right-wing nutjobs' bandwagon of discrimination and exclusion of minorities they resented and made no effort to understand? And what in the sam-hell were they doing living in a damn trailer park?

I didn't know. But one thing I *did* know, and that was that Lance was going to pay for his cruelty and abuse, and he was going to pay *dearly*. For Lance, gay though he might be, had committed an unpardonable sin: he criticized Boo and Sully's unfortunate behavior.

The next night, Smoky Joe's party was in full swing. We could hear glasses clinking and the occasional clapping of hands. It was hard to tell, but the party-goers seemed to be taking turns speaking, possibly toasting a guest of honor.

It was a mild, pleasant evening, and me and my old man let Boo and Sully outside to sit with us on our newly-finished, gated deck. We replenished our glasses from a full box of wine on the table between us, and waved at many passersby. As was their custom, Sully and Boo barked and screeched at every one of them long after they were out of sight.

Around 9pm or so, the Joes' party was breaking up, and we polished off the rest of the wine, put the dogs in the trailer, and prepared to go inside ourselves.

As we were doing so, a good-looking young guy walked up the path to our deck and introduced himself as a local Democrat, running for office in the state legislature to replace the lunatic Republican incumbent we both detested. We shook his hand and promised him our vote. As he was leaving, he stopped and turned around.

"By the way, I should tell you that Lance and Wade spoke very highly of you at my fund raiser tonight. They said that having you as their neighbors was the best thing that's happened to them in years. We're so glad you're a part of our progressive community."

We went back inside the trailer, and I unleashed the spigot on another box of wine while my old man disposed of a clutch of anonymous dog turds from the area rug. It seemed like our period of adjustment living at Oceanview was going to take a little longer than previously anticipated. And I guessed, after all these years, I was still "queer bait."

Homeless Andy

After the fund raiser and my old man's characteristic misreading of Lance's good intentions toward our dogs, we patched things up by gifting the Joes with a hammock we'd bought six months earlier, but had never used.

The gift accomplished two things: it got rid of a tippy, uncomfortable lounger we didn't really have room for, and it provided a trampoline for their 7-year old bratski who bounced up and down on it instead of clomping around on their deck all day long.

Another good thing about having Lance and Wade as neighbors was that they had a rather nice 28' motor home they kept stored in town, and they used it – a lot. Winters, they traveled southward, home-schooling Matt and seeing the sights.

They spent summers at Oceanview, but very often they took 2 or 3-day trips - or even longer - to visit relatives and friends back east. So we didn't have to put up with them for long stretches at a time.

I learned that it was Wade who was the smoker in their family. Lance was very disapproving of the habit, and wouldn't allow smoking inside their trailers or vehicles.

"I married a human smokestack," he told me. "I dearly love the man, but his smoking has driven me away more than once, and I worry myself sick about the effect his secondhand smoke is having on Matt and me, and the dogs."

I had no idea how Lance and Wade supported themselves, although Lance told me that he was a commercial artist, and that Wade had retired from teaching a few years previous. Wade was obviously the older of the two, but Lance's age was indeterminable.

Both men were devoted to Matt, who I found out sometime later was the unwanted child of one of their unmarried relatives. They planned to tell him about his biological parents when he was old enough, but at the moment they were concentrating on giving him as carefree a childhood as they could provide. As annoying as he was, the kid was as happy and well-adjusted as any I'd ever known.

In addition to Lance and Wade, we got to know a few other residents of Oceanview. The manager of the park, Adrian, was one of the first. When she was drinking, Adrian was the most likable, friendliest person around. When she was on the wagon, she was a she-demon straight from hell.

Thankfully, Adrian drank most of the time, and to be honest, it was Oceanview residents who made sure her liquor cabinet was always well-stocked. She had her own list of "enemies," and Stan Carlyle's name was at the top of it.

"You wouldn't believe the aggravation that man's caused me," she confided to me one day. "He thinks he's exempt from all the park rules because he's been here so long, and he won't keep his site clean no matter what."

"He parks his shitty truck at other people's sites whether they're there or not, and God help me, when he uses the bathroom in the clubhouse, it takes Richie and Tim (her two adult sons who were part of the maintenance staff) two hours to fumigate it and hose down the shower."

She paused for a long sip of something from a coffee mug. The mug had *"To answer your question, Go Fuck Yourself"* printed on one side.

"I'll tell you something else about Stan Carlyle," Adrian said, stretching her neck until I heard a distinct crack. "He doesn't keep up with his dues. A couple times we've almost had to evict him before he finally wrote out a check and got caught up."

"He's got money, but he's a real tightwad about paying his bills and all. The only reason he still lives here at Oceanview is because he thinks he's going to sell that junky site and his nasty trailer for a million dollars one of these days."

Adrian chuckled and took another pull at her *Go fuck yourself* mug. We've put up with his shit for a long time, all because of his wife. She's an invalid, and Stan's all the family she's got left." I admitted we hadn't met Stan's wife yet or even caught sight of her.

"It's an ordeal for her to get around, and Stan whines and carries on about how much trouble it is for *him*, the old bastard. She used to have a nice flower garden and she was the one who kept their site cleaned up, but that arthritis finally got the best of her, poor little thing. Lonnie May doesn't hardly ever come out of their trailer anymore except to go to the doctor."

I froze. For a brief second I thought I might faint. **It. Could. Not. Be.**

"Wait a minute, Adrian, did you just say Stan's wife's name is 'Lonnie May'?" Adrian sat back and stared at me blankly. She was already three sheets to the wind.

"Oh hell no!" she said, roaring with laughter. "Lonnie's a *man's* name, and Lottie ain't no Lesbian. Her name's *Lottie May*. Lottie May Carlyle."

I knew it now for sure. Lightning had definitely struck twice in our own back yard. Only the yards were in different trailer parks. Stan Carlyle *was* Lonnie May, and Adrian *was* Virginia Lopp.

Adrian said we might want to meet Steve and Lisa, a retired couple who'd moved from land-locked Nebraska to be near the ocean. She said they were a very religious pair, and were active in the Baptist church, so I immediately scratched them from my list of potential chums.

Another retired couple who'd moved to Oceanview about the same time we had, were John and JoAnne. They'd come all the way from South Carolina, and according to Adrian it was to get as far away from their crazy hillbilly relatives as possible.

They sounded more our style, but I was a little concerned about their last name, which was "Fuchs." I wasn't entirely sure I'd be able to avert a pants-pissing if their surname was spoken out loud when I was around.

As we closed in on some of the more complicated trailer and yard projects, we had more free time to explore the little beachside community outside the park.

We took Boo and Sully on walks along the shore, and they galloped and pranced and generally had a great time until they spotted other humans or dogs or an ant, at which time they'd commence whooping and screeching until even the roar of the ocean wasn't enough to overshadow the din.

We decided to leave them at home rather than throttle their asses or expose them to thoughtless criticism from other beach walkers.

More than anything, we wanted to adapt to the lifestyle and customs of our new community, which brings me to the story of the "the beard." And by "beard," I don't mean the middle-aged gal who tags along behind Lindsey Graham when he's in Washington, DC. I'm talking about the facial hair now covering my old man's saggy jowls.

Not long after we moved to Oceanview, my old man noticed that a majority of other geezers in the area have beards, some so bushy and frightening, when they walk into the local pawn shop, the husky female owner keeps one hand on her pistol under the counter.

Desperate to conform to the customs of other hep cats of his generation, he decided to grow a beard of his own. The scraggly brush *does* cover a multitude of sins, and he doesn't have to shave his upper lip once a week. That, I freely admit, makes me a wee bit jealous.

I was also eager to adopt the prevailing trends among Oceanview's womenfolk, so I continued to cut my own hair while drunk. It looks awful, but no worse than other women around here who cut their own hair while sober. And macular degeneration significantly levels the playing field for all concerned.

So anyways, we were both doing everything we could think of to fit into the community, including leaving our turn signals on for six blocks, and remaining stopped at intersections for two or three minutes after the traffic light turned green. It was a struggle, but we persisted.

We hung out at McDonalds, where members of the local geezerhood congregated in their Buicks and PT Cruiser hotrods, and it was while sitting in the parking lot at Mickey D's that I first noticed Homeless Andy.

I was waiting for my old man to fetch me a sausage McMuffin, when I observed a geezerly man sitting in a wheel chair at the corner. Actually, it wasn't a wheel chair so much as it was a car seat that had been converted into a chair with wheels.

The old man in the chair was well dressed and cheerful, as he waved at passersby and held up a sign. I couldn't read what it said from my vantage point, but I was impressed by the number of people who stopped to hand money to the old fellow; some even passed wrapped burgers and McMuffins to him, which he gratefully accepted and scarfed down as his benefactors drove off.

As we left the parking lot, the folks in the car in front of us stopped to pass him some cash, and I was able to read his sign:

Homeless Andy!

Need $ for gas & food!

God Bless!

Each time we went to McDonald's thereafter, I saw Homeless Andy sitting in his wheeled car seat on the corner, waving and holding up his sign. He did quite a good business, and I admired the ingenuity of his rolling "office" chair, which looked really comfortable.

I couldn't help but feel sorry for him, though. Stove up like that and homeless - I wondered where the poor old guy slept at night – maybe in a tent somewhere on the beach, or hidden in the bushes along the highway. Only God knew.

One afternoon as I was waiting for my McNuggets, it started to rain. It was a gentle sprinkle at first, then turned into a heavy downpour. I watched with fascination as Homeless Andy got out of his chair, tucked the God Bless sign under his jacket, and walked off, pulling the chair behind him.

He headed across the parking lot and stopped beside a fairly late model pickup truck (newer than ours) that was towing a trailer of about 25 feet. He hoisted the chair over the side and into the bed of the truck, and I was awe-struck at the strength and dexterity of the man. He then walked to the door of the trailer, unlocked it, and went inside.

The rain continued, and we ate our lunch and left without seeing Homeless Andy emerge from his trailer. My guess was that he was either napping or using McDonald's wifi to surf the net until things dried up and the sun came back out.

From that moment on, when we went to McDonald's, I looked for Homeless Andy's trailer. Sometimes it was there, and sometimes just his truck was in the parking lot. It appeared that "Homeless Andy" wasn't exactly homeless, except for the days he left his "home" at a trailer park.

A lot of panhandlers passed through town, and all of them congregated near shopping areas or at the entrance to grocery store parking lots.

I never saw any that weren't fairly well-dressed-at least as good as we were – and many of them were accompanied by overweight dogs of indiscriminate breeds, who sat mournfully on a towel or blanket, head on paws, helping their master bring in enough cash for dinner and whatever.

Most of the beggars carried the same "equipment"- hefty backpacks and multiple signs with various reasons for needing a handout. The signs I saw most frequently were "Stranded! No gas! Please help!" or "Need money for sick child."

On one occasion I spied on a strapping young beggar whose "Stranded!" sign and fat dog didn't seem to be working for him. I watched as he removed a marker from his jacket and wrote "God Bless" below his plea for help.

Almost immediately a car stopped and money was passed through the passenger's window. When we pulled out of the parking lot and up to the stop sign, I sat there speechless while my old man motioned the guy over and handed him a fiver.

"What in the hell were you thinking? He's working a con!"

My old man shrugged like the bleeding heart pushover he is. "It was *for the dog*. Did you see its sad little face?"

On another occasion I watched a group of panhandlers taking turns holding up their pitiful signs, and frequently breaking for a smoke in one of the group member's cars.

Those were the ones that really pissed me off, especially when I saw a sign at the drugstore advertising the price for *one pack* of Marlboros at $9.56. Damned if I was going to pay for them to get cancer from smoking, and then help foot the bill for their hospice care.

I was spending a lot of time protesting Trump's callous agenda, and at the same time I was worried that my own heart might be turning to stone.

What did it matter if a few panhandlers got by hoodwinking people out of a couple lousy bucks on weekends when the insatiably greedy guy in the White House conned millions of Americans out of their savings and their healthcare every day of the week?

The beggars' petty misdemeanors paled in comparison to the out-and-out fraud taking place in our own government. At least when it came to panhandlers, we all had a choice as to whether we wanted to contribute.

I'd envisioned Oceanview as a compassionate, caring refuge for Progressives like me and my old man, and a welcome escape from the hellish heat and mean-spirited conservatism of the desert southwest. Now I was beginning to think we'd made a terrible mistake moving here. Well, at least my old man had.

Maybe living in the middle of nowhere in the desert and our life at The Resort hadn't been so bad after all. We'd forged several interesting friendships there, and even Lonnie May, with his devotion to Daisy May, wasn't quite as repulsive as Stan Carlyle.

And, as I recalled, there weren't as many drunkards and misfits - except for me and Virginia Lopp – at The Resort as there were at Oceanview, probably because it didn't rain all the damn time and wasn't as depressing.

And Ben was alive when were at The Resort. That was the best part. What was happening to me? Was I homesick for Hell?

THE MORAL OF THE STORY

The grass is always greener on the other side of the fence. Especially when you forget that there wasn't any grass on the other side of the fence, just a concrete slab surrounded by sunburned weeds, prickly pear spines, and a wrecked Cornhole Court.

14 - WELCOME BACK TO HELL

I am literally starting to write this chapter at *The Gates of Hell*. The gates are merely decorative, and do not open or close. They frame both sides of Hell's blacktop driveway, and the gate on the left has a sign affixed to it that says "Welcome Back Home!"

We have never stayed at this RV park before, and wouldn't stay here again if Ninja Warriors held their long sharp knives to our throats and slapped our faces with their bare feet, so we don't feel particularly sentimental about the effusive greeting.

The park itself is huge, and consists of permanent park model trailers, UV-ravaged motor homes, 5th wheel and regular travel trailers crammed in cheek-to-jowl on a treeless terrain. Me and my old man, Boo and Sully, are housed in our 23' travel trailer, which is clearly the smallest dwelling in the park.

Among other features, the park has an itty bitty swimming pool with no cabana or shade, a hot tub that's near boiling, a dingy laundry room, and a "clubhouse" that's always empty. An airport is nearby, and round-the-clock take offs and landings are drowned out only by the constant roar of the freeway and an on-ramp that are within spitting distance of our site.

We're in town to town to transfer a few assets, and plan to stay for a month or so while my old man finishes up some IT projects he's been working on. He's going to tell his employers (for whom he's been working via telecommute from Oceanview) that he's retiring *for good*.

We will not be returning to Hell in the foreseeable future, unless passing through on our way to a winter getaway anywhere but here.

Weeks ago, when I called The Resort to reserve a site, Laurette Lopp, who is now running the place, said they didn't have anything available for at least three months, and that she couldn't guarantee us a site even then.

Every decent spot at The Resort was booked for the season, and the only options open were Good Sam overnight sites that went for $50. We passed, deciding that $1580 was too expensive for one month in a park that was 40 minutes away from my old man's office.

Since we would have only the pickup truck with us, I'd be without transportation during the day while my old man was at work, and the cost of gas for his roundtrip commute would be astronomical.

While I chatted with Laurette, she filled me in on certain changes at The Resort. The most interesting to me involved her Mom, Virginia, who'd been my closest friend there.

Virginia is in her 80's, and lived in a park model at The Resort for years, with Laurette on one side in another park model, and her other daughter, Claudia, in a park model on the other side.

When Virginia bought half interest in The Resort from its Canadian owners, Laurette had taken over management of the office. Claudia, not inclined to hang around the park all day, had found a job at the sheriff's office as a dispatcher.

Weeks before we moved from The Resort to Oceanview, Virginia was in California visiting her sister. While she was there, she met her sister's 60-something widowed neighbor and struck up a romantic relationship with him. Now the two lovebirds were living together in drunken sin, according to Laurette.

"Brownie's a really nice man," she informed me. "But he's not that good-looking, and I'm sure Mom's just after his money. I hope he doesn't let her con him into getting married."

"What about Princess?" I asked, fearing that Virginia, in a drunken haze, had forgotten about her beloved Persian cat and had left her behind. I shouldn't have worried.

"Oh, Mom and Brownie came and picked Princess up on their way to Vegas two months ago. And Mom sold her park model - to Gerald. He and Lulu are living right next door to me now."

I was *stunned*. Maybe not as stunned as General Kelly when he realized he wasn't up to the job of babysitting a full grown orange shitgibbon at the White house, but stunned nonetheless.

"But Gerald bought our 5th wheel…I thought he was going to live in it."

"Well, he *was*," Laurette continued, "But then Mom gave him a good price on her park model, and he just couldn't resist. He would have moved in with me, but his Lulu is still real jealous of our relationship and all, and we thought we should give her more time to adjust."

Lulu was Gerald's grossly overweight, bossy, Bichon Frise. She was adorable, but also very strict when it came to sharing Gerald with anyone else. In that regard, she was a lot like Lonnie's Daisy May.

"So what did Gerald do with our 5th wheel?" I asked.

Laurette laughed. "You'll *love* this: He sold your trailer to Lonnie May, and Lonnie sold *his* trailer to a friend of his. Lonnie's been working off the rest of what he owes Gerald by doing odd jobs around the park."

"So he and Gerald finally buried the hatchet?" That was hard to imagine, as the two had never gotten along.

"Gerald would *like* to bury the hatchet, alright. *In Lonnie's skull.* Lonnie gripes non-stop about everything, and half the time he doesn't do what Gerald asks him to. They argue a lot. Just this morning Lonnie said he wouldn't be able to weed-whack today because Daisy May ate something off the ground and got the runs. He uses that excuse all the time."

Laurette went on to say that Bill Crane had suffered another heart attack, and had to have two more stents put in. He was doing fine, but he and Phyllis had decided not come back to the park this year. Neither one of them felt like they were up to the long trip.

I hadn't communicated with Phyllis in ages, mainly because I hadn't wanted to tell her about Ben's death. Bill had become quite attached to him and Sully during our walks around the park, and I was kind of relieved, not just that Bill was doing ok, but that I didn't have to break the sad news to him.

Cripple Jon had also made headlines, Laurette told me. His photo had appeared on the front page of The Resort's new community bulletin under the headline: **PARK RESIDENT THANKS PRESIDENT**. She mailed me a copy of the article, which, as editor and publisher of the bulletin, she'd written herself.

In a photo accompanying the article, Jon's sitting in his wheelchair, a smug grin on his face and wearing a Make America Great Again cap - either the same one he'd managed to retrieve from Daisy May, or a new one.

The article states that Jon has found a part time job at a bowling alley near town, where he hands out rented shoes and bowling balls. He's quoted as saying he owes his employment to President Trump for "bringing good jobs back to America."

"You'd think he owns the place," Laurette huffed. "He *will not* shut up about that damn bowling alley for two minutes. When I see him rolling toward the office, I run and hide in the restroom until he leaves. There's just so much you want to hear about sanitizing shoes and reaming out finger holes in bowling balls."

"How about Dottie Ballou?" I asked. "Did Dottie ever sell her 5th wheel over by the cornhole stadium?"

"She sure did," Laurette said. "Sold it to a Canadian couple. They bought it for her asking price. Didn't haggle at all. I think I heard somebody say Dottie's in Michigan or somewhere up north on an extended hunting trip right now. You know what a gun nut she is."

"Yep, she was really pissed when the County wouldn't let you guys convert the cornhole stadium into a shooting range. That's why she moved to an apartment."

"I know…" Laurette acknowledged wistfully. "She'd *really* shit a load of bricks if she saw it now. The Canadian couple and a bunch of their friends turned the Cornhole court into a Pickleball court. They took up a collection to pay for it and did all the work themselves. All the old folks around here have signed up to play Pickleball. Gerald and I play too. It's a blast."

Pickleball..? I'd never heard of it. It sure didn't sound Canadian to me. German maybe, but then wouldn't it be called *Kraut Ball*? Canada had nothing to do with pickles, as far as I knew, and the sport certainly couldn't have originated in Canada, where Professional Cornholing had virtually replaced Ice Hockey as the national obsession.

It sounded to me more like another case of Canadians stealing American technology and trying to take credit for the superior athletic skills of our black athletes. Hell, I'd never seen a Canadian *eating* a pickle, let alone playing with one. Then I recalled a poem I'd read somewhere years before....

There once was a lad named McDurkin
Who insisted on jerkin' his gherkin
His mum said, McDurkin!
Stop jerkin' yer gherkin
Yer gherkin's fer ferkin', not jerkin'

Now that I thought about it, the "mum" and the "ferkin"in the verse *did* sound like language a Canadian, still slavishly faithful to the British crown, might use. It all seemed very strange and possibly treasonous to me.

"Well, it's great that geezers in the park have something more to do than sit around on their fat asses and whine about Obama taking their guns away," I remarked.

As soon as the words were out of my mouth I regretted them. Like Dottie Ballou, Gerald Karn, Laurette's *Significant Other,* was a huge gun nut and an avid hunter. The sheep horns and deer antlers Gerald kept piled up around his trailer had been a source of pride for him, not to mention supplemental income, thanks to the less successful trophy hunters who bought them from him.

Gerald had been among the most vocal of opponents to the idea of banning guns from The Resort, and he was an ardent supporter of the Gun Range versus Cornhole Stadium proposal.

Also, Laurette was a geezer herself, and she had a pretty fat ass. I liked her and hoped my candor and innocent fat-shaming hadn't insulted her. She didn't let on if she was offended by the faux pas.

Despite her otherwise placid and dog-loving personality, she was a backward, Trump-leaning woman, and it was highly likely she didn't know what a "faux pas" was. I doubted she was savvy enough to google its meaning and correct spelling on the computer as I had.

"Well, there *was* a commotion over the Pickleball Court - at first," Laurette said, interrupting my thoughts.

"It all started because everybody wanted to use the court at the same time, in the mornings before it got too hot. There were some death threats made and some gunplay, but Gerald finally calmed folks down by threatening to shut it down altogether. Then he banned guns from the park entirely, and there hasn't been any more trouble since."

"Everybody loves Pickleball!" she said with uncustomary enthusiasm. "It's really brought us all together like nothing else has."

I was gob-smacked. Gerald, of all people had banned guns at The Resort? And the geezers were now busy playing Pickleball instead of 'Trash-Obama-Even-Though-He-Didn't-Take-Our-Fucking-Guns-And-Isn't-President-Anymore'?

I shook my head in wonderment. Bob Dylan had been such a visionary when he wrote *The Times They are a Changin'* back in 1965, which was long before I was even born, and why I had to look up who he was and what kind of songs he wrote so I could put them in this book all these years later because you people are too lazy to do your own goddamn research on these matters.

Anyhow, *whoever* Bob Dylan was, even *he* would have been freaked on his ass to learn that residents of The Resort had actually found something they all liked and agreed on. I told Laurette we'd definitely drive out to The Resort for a visit when we got back in town. I had to see the miracles for myself.

After my conversation with Laurette, I cracked open a fresh box of wine, siphoned off a tumbler full, and started calling other RV parks closer in to Helltown.

After the box was almost half empty, I found a park with an available site the month we'd be there. It was only 10 minutes from my old man's office, convenient to shopping and budget-priced at $550 for one month, not including electricity.

The name of the park was "Villaggio Paradiso." It sounded ideal and romantic, and in the pictures on the website it did indeed look like an RVer's paradise. Not wanting to lose out on such a fantastic deal, I booked a month's stay and made a non-refundable deposit with our debit card.

A couple weeks later when we arrived at Villaggio Paradiso, it didn't look a thing like the pictures on the website. A prickly geezer in a golf cart directed us to our site, which was squeezed in between a dated park model and a square-fronted "eyebrow" Winnebago motor home that probably hadn't been road-worthy since 1974.

We'd no sooner got parked and "dropped anchor," when a frizzy-haired geezer woman with a beer in one hand came traipsing through our space as though completely unaware she was committing the deadliest of all sins at RV campgrounds.

"Don't mind me, I'm just passing through," she called, saluting us with the beer bottle and a wide, partly toothless grin. Boo and Sully went wild, screeching at the intrusion, and neither of us acknowledged the woman's pitiful attempt at pleasantry.

It was evident that yet again, my old man had used atrocious judgment when he turned over complicated RV park reservations to me when I'd been drinking. For, if one of us was going to royally fuck up in these matters, it was always going to be *him*.

Life in Village Helladiso

Living at Villaggio Paradiso wasn't actually as bad as I had thought it would be when we first got there. It was FAR FUCKING worse.

The weather was hot and dry, and my chronic Dry Eye Syndrome was driving me insane. I used moisture-restoring eye drops all day long, and no matter if I squirted a quart in each eye every five minutes, my eyelids still felt like two sheets of sandpaper.

Adding to my misery was the diesel-fueled air pollution coming from the constant traffic on the nearby freeway. Evenings, everyone cooked outside, and smoke from all the grills swirled around our little trailer in fetid clouds of charred pig, cow, and chicken grease fumes.

Right away, we realized we were going to have to turn on the AC and leave it on all the time if we were to survive our stay in "paradise." The constant drizzle and chilly air at Oceanview was starting to sound pretty good.

While my old man spent his day in a high-rise, air-conditioned office, I spent mine trying to write and keep myself and the dogs comfortable.

I took Boo and Sully for walks to the ends of the park three times a day, where they hurriedly did their business in fenced "pet stations" that smelled so awful, sometimes I had to use one of their poop bags to gag into. When we got back to the trailer, I held them outside to disinfect their paws and muzzles.

Both of them hated the park, with its nasty smells and unsavory dog and cat population that spied on them from behind curtained trailer windows, never failing to catch their attention and sending them into fits of screechery outrage during our walks.

To mitigate their misery (and mine), I stocked up on several bags of Pork Chomp chews and stockpiled a month's worth of box wine in the trailer's tiny shower. It was a chore moving the wine each time I showered, but due to my old man's lack of common sense, I had little choice in the matter.

Residents of the park were mostly geezers who never left their sites except to do laundry or take their dogs to the canine shit zones, and they did so from air-conditioned comfort.

As I approached a station each morning with Boo and Sully, an idling car would usually be parked close to the fenced station, a man or woman sitting inside while their dog - or dogs - pissed and shat.

Its tasks complete, the dog would walk through the left-open gate and hop into the waiting car. Dog and master would then speed off without disposing of the fresh steaming turds, already attracting flies in the morning sun. The offenders would rush back home to their trailer or 5th wheel, which was usually parked a block away. Nobody walked anywhere in the park…except us.

One afternoon, nauseated by the stench at the closest dog station, I led Boo and Sully in the opposite direction to get their exercise in a deserted area reserved for storing RVs. Almost immediately, a thin, sharp-featured witch in a golf cart pulled in front of us, blocking our path.

"You're not allowed in this area. There are dog comfort stations at each end of the park," she scolded, indicating the direction of the stations like a flight attendant pointing out emergency exits on a plane.

"We're trying to keep our park clean and sanitary, and we would appreciate it if you would use the stations instead of letting your dogs roam at large."

Terrorized by the golf cart, which they didn't register as dog *or* human, Boo and Sully stood in uncharacteristic silence beside me.

Fearing that I was about to lose my temper and might strip the woman's tonsils from her throat with my bare teeth, I made no reply. Instead, I turned around and led Boo and Sully back the way we'd come.

Behind us, I heard clunking and grinding noises, and what I thought was muttered profanity. I glanced back and saw that the witch's golf cart was experiencing a mechanical malfunction. The cart jerked forward a foot or so, then clattered loudly before coming to an abrupt halt.

After a number of failed attempts to get the uncooperative golf cart moving reliably, the woman hopped out, snatched an armful of loose papers from the seat, and appeared to be power-walking back toward the office.

She stopped to pick up a few papers she'd dropped, and it was then I noticed her hopping about as she retrieved the scattered documents. She was *barefoot*, and the sizzling pavement was scorching the bottoms of her lily-white feet.

I should have ignored the comical scene, but my better angels took command. Letting go of the intense anger I'd felt moments before, I bent over, picked up Boo and Sully, tucking each under an arm, and carried them quickly over the hot pavement all the way back to our trailer.

The back pain that ensued as a result of my selfless act of Christian charity was somewhat moderated by the knowledge that the she-devil's cloven hooves were probably burned to a crisp.

THE MORAL OF THE STORY

Hell can get extremely hot, especially if the people in charge of it are assholes.

15 - JUST VISITING

On a Saturday, toward the end of our self-imposed month stay in Helltown, we packed a lunch, put Boo and Sully in the truck, and headed off to The Resort. We were both anxious to see the new Canadian Pickleball court and pay a short visit to our old stomping grounds.

When we got there, Laurette was tied up with a couple geezers inquiring about purchasing one of the Resort-owned park models. She waved to acknowledge my presence, and I used sign language to indicate to her that we'd drive around the park and catch up with her later.

We first drove over to the three Lopp park models, which were pretty much the same as they had been, except for the one in the middle that now belonged to Gerald Karn.

Virginia Lopp's once-tidy site was strewn with sheep horns and antlers, and the chairs and tables on her small porch had been replaced by rakes, shovels and other grounds keeping equipment, along with several rusted barbecue grills.

I was thrilled to see Lulu, the fat little Bichon, perched on the back of a sofa, her white curly head bobbing as she kept watch on the traffic outside her window. Even at that distance I could tell Lulu hadn't lost any weight, but she was still perfectly groomed and cute as hell.

Laurette's park model was on the other side of Gerald's, and her colorful menagerie of plastic bunnies, squirrels and gnomes still frolicked on a tiny patch of artificial turf. Compared to Gerald's site, Laurette's looked as though it had been professionally landscaped.

Claudia Lopp's trailer was pristine as usual, and the space around it was raked, swept, with not a cactus spine out of place. The air conditioners in all three trailers were humming, and there was no sign of the Lopp girls' dogs that I'd once thought about dognapping, in addition to Lulu.

We continued on past the Canadian section of the park, passing by a row of well-kept, expensive rigs, with their maple leaf flags and windsocks fluttering weakly in a light breeze. I experienced a momentary fit of jealousy, thinking about the Canucks' big fancy RVs, their universal healthcare, and their sane, intelligent, good-looking Prime Minister, Justin Trudeau.

Back at the entrance to The Resort, Phyllis and Bill's park model sat empty, their shrubs and bushes overgrown and dropping leaves on the patio. The windows of the Crane trailer were still lined with reflective insulation material they'd taped up before leaving the previous year, and Bill's golf cart was parked in the middle of their patio, wrapped tightly in a canvas cover.

I couldn't help but recall the many times I'd walked Ben and Sully past their spot and Bill had called us over for treats, a cold drink, and his profanity-laced rant about the incompetence of every person he'd ever hired to do work inside or outside their trailer. The bittersweet memory made me choke up.

We turned the corner and proceeded down to our old site at the end of the row. Parked in our former spot was a 40' motor home with a huge slide-out that was infringing upon "free space" on its far side. Gretchen Bird, the former manager of The Resort, would have issued an immediate complaint notice, and would have levied a fine had she been there to assess the extent of the violation.

Just beyond the motor home, the new Pickleball court stood resplendent in all its glory. And I had to admit, it *was* an impressive sight. Actually, it consisted of *three* courts of the same size, maybe 20 by 50 feet each. There were nets in the middle of the courts, and the blue surface they were laid out on was striped, sort of like a tennis court.

Canadian and American flags were displayed side by side at the entrance to the fields of play, and teams of geezers were on each of the courts, armed with short-handled paddles with solid heads.

The paddles were shaped more like small pizza paddles than tennis rackets. Even though it was warm out, none of the players – a mix of sheezers and heezers - looked worse for the wear. They were laughing and appeared to be having a good time.

A couple of park benches were placed outside the arena, and geezers waiting for an open court were chatting amicably. They waved at us as we drove by, and it was impossible to tell just from looking at them whether they were American or Canadian. We really needed to put a system in place to identify Canadians on sight, and make them pay for it.

Dottie Ballou's 5th wheel, now sporting a Canadian maple leaf flag, was parked in the same spot, next to the Pickleball courts. The new owner (a Canadian) had set up a table with a large water cooler on top and a stack of paper cups. A hand-made sign said "Everybody welcome - help yourself, please."

My old man stopped, and I got out and filled Boo and Sully's plastic bowl with fresh water, probably drawn from a Canadian sink tap deep in the Rockies.

We pulled around the corner, and there was our old 5th wheel, now parked at Lonnie May's site. It was streaked with dirt and needed waxing, and Lonnie May's utility trailer and half-size pickup truck barely fit in beside it.

He'd used the lumber we'd left behind to build wooden steps up to the door, and they were painted a hideous shade of blue-green, probably from a can he'd scavenged from somewhere. We were surprised to see Lonnie sitting at his picnic table with Daisy at his feet.

My old man stopped the truck again, and I rolled down the window and called out to Lonnie. He looked up, puzzled, and did a double take. When he realized who we were, he got up from the picnic table and hobbled over to the truck, Daisy May limping along behind him.

Lonnie's filthy red cap was missing and his balding head was sunburned and surrounded by long, greasy wisps of hair. He was wearing a Bernie Sanders T-shirt, which was very likely the same shirt that had belonged to my old man, and which I had tossed in the park dumpster before we moved.

He had on a pair of wrinkled and stained shorts, and his legs were still knotted and painful looking. My old man held Sully and

Boo's heads down so they wouldn't see Daisy May and start a commotion when Lonnie walked up to chat.

"Well, lookie here, wontcha, Daisy May, it's our old neighbors come to call. And they brung that little shit Sully along too! Now, who's this cute little white guy?" he wanted to know, reaching through the window to pet Boo, who scrunched in closer to Sully and growled at the stranger.

"Where's that old Ben hidin'?" he wanted to know. I told him about Ben's death, and he visibly winced and hung his head.

"Son of a bitch," he blurted. "I *hate* to hear that. He was a good little ol' boy.

"There ain't nothin' much can be done about it when they git old like that. My Daisy's goin' on 16, and she's laid up about half the time with one thing or another. She got into some garbage the other day and got the shits real bad. I tell you, it was one fuckin' mess, that's what it was, wasn't it Daisy May? Your old Dad was up all night cleanin' your runs, wasn't he girlie?"

Daisy looked away, acknowledging Lonnie's comments with a disinterested wag of her stumpy tail. She seemed nonplussed by her old dad's revelation of the unfortunate incidents. Lonnie steadied himself, putting both hands, minus his missing fingers, on the edge of the truck's window. I noticed his hands were covered with puncture wounds and deep red welts.

"What's going on with your hands, Lonnie? "They look like you've been fighting a tiger."

Lonnie guffawed. "I reckon they do look all tored up, don't they? Daisy May had her a bad tooth that had to come out. She wouldn't hardly eat nothin' and her breath was like cat shit on a hot day. That tooth was all wobbly and nasty, and finely I just grabbed aholt of her head and reached in there and yanked it out. She's all healed up now, but I think some of them bites she gave me is infected."

"You need to put something on those right away," I advised him. "They look bad."

"Yeah, I probbly should get my ass to the doctor for some medicine, but money's been purty tight since Trump got in. Everthing's costin' more and I can't afford to take Daisy May to the vets no more. That Trump don't care nothin' about vets, though. I seen it on the TV! He's nothin' but a big fuckin' coward with his hill spurs and his draft dodgin' the Viet war and all. He's tryin' to take ar Medicare and ar Social Security, and them republicans is helpin' him do it!"

I sat back in the seat and shook my head briskly to try and wake myself up. It had to be true. Space aliens had landed with their brain-washing pods and had taken over The Resort.

The pods had turned all the narrow-minded, violence-prone geezers into pleasant, friendly Canadians. Except for Lonnie May, who had mutated into a bleeding heart liberal. Lonnie was getting more and more agitated talking about Trump, so I changed the subject.

"How do you like living in our trailer, Lonnie? I see you built yourself some steps for it."

Lonnie backed away a little from the truck and ran his chewed up, finger-deficient hand through his straggly hair. "Well, now, not all that lumber was sold as advertised." he said, seeming to forget that he hadn't paid a nickel for it.

"I had to toss out some of it and replace it with stuff I had in the shed. But I reckon it turned out ok after I painted it up." He paused and thought for a second, then went on.

"Now, that trailer is a different horse collar. I paid old Gerald a pretty penny for that thing, and it ain't worth it. It's all wored out inside and it don't smell too good in there neither."

"Do you think the smell might be from Daisy May's diarrhea?"

"Oh *hell* no!" Lonnie shot back, offended right down to his hills. "I cleaned that mess up with a warsh rag and vinegar water. That smell was there when I bought the thing. I think his Lulu mighta taken a shit or two in there and old Gerald just left it be. He's a real asshole. *Did you know that*?"

I didn't answer, remembering Ben's "frequent accidents" in "the thing." And anyway, I'd steam-cleaned the carpets before we'd moved, and I knew damn well the smell wasn't from either of our dogs. I thought it was time to move along.

"Lonnie, it's been really great seeing you again," I lied. "I'm glad you and Daisy May are still here and getting by ok."

"Well, I wisht we *was*…gettin' by, that is," Lonnie began. "My Social's done been spent, and what with my infected bit hand and all, and needin' to get some medicine for it, I probably ain't gonna be able to make rent next month. Gerald won't cut me no slack on payin' him back for that trailer of your-alls neither"

Lonnie sighed deeply and shrugged. "A lot of work needs to be done on that thing before it's hospitable. I'm just a hard up workin' man who can't barely afford to keep his poor old dog fed." He sniffed and hung his head, and I thought he might be crying. Daisy May moved closer and looked up at him with sorrowful eyes.

I had appreciated his kind words about Ben. He'd called Sully a "little shit" again, but he was smiling when he said it, and it sounded vaguely affectionate. I found myself feeling sorry for the wretch, despite his big know-it-all mouth and absurd posturing. He loved his dog and would do anything for her, including debase himself however much sniveling it took.

So, there I was, reaching for my purse and pulling out a twenty for the scrounger while my old man looked on and mouthed the word "sucker." Lonnie was pleased with the offering.

"See this girlie," he said, waving the twenty at Daisy May. "Now yer ol' Dad can buy a couple steaks for our supper and have enough left over for a scratcher or two."

We started to drive away, but Lonnie raised a three-fingered hand, signaling he had a final word for us. I rolled down the window and he stuck his big dirty face in close. "God bless," he said, before he turned and walked away.

The last I saw of him and Daisy May, they were in Lonnie's truck, racing off to forage for steaks and lottery tickets.

My old man shook his head in disgust. "What the hell were you thinking, giving that bum twenty bucks? He's a con man, and he uses Daisy May to make you feel sorry for him."

I had to agree. All that my old man said about Lonnie was true. He *was* a bum and a con man, and not only that, he was one of the most aggravating, narcissistic people I'd ever run into. But he *had* seemed genuinely sympathetic about our loss of Ben, and anyways, I'd already given him the twenty and it was too late to ask for it back.

"When you're right, you're right," I sighed. "But you know, without Lonnie and Daisy May and the rest of the batshit loons at The Resort, *Trailer Dogs* might have been just another boring flop like *War and Peace*. Besides, the twenty was for Daisy May. Did you see her sad little face?"

My old man didn't have a workable response, so he headed toward the office so I could say goodbye to Laurette. She was still talking with the geezer couple, but she broke away from their conversation and came over to give me a big hug.

"God, I wish Mom was here to see you! She asks about you every time I talk to her. In fact, she called last night and told me to be sure and tell you she said hello. She also said to tell you that her and Brownie might drop in on you at Oceanview next year. They're talking about buying a motor home with an arctic insulation package, and Mom said if Brownie gets his license back, they're going to drive it to Alaska."

Laurette paused. "To tell you the truth, though, I think Mom was drunk when she said it." The geezer couple was getting antsy, and Laurette gave me a final hug before going back to their pow wow.

On the way out of The Resort we saw Gerald Karn, high up on an extension ladder, sawing dead fronds off a palm tree. We hadn't talked to him during our visit, but I cautioned my old man against a goodbye honk and a wave that might distract him and cause him to fall. "We don't want to make Lulu an orphan," I said, momentarily forgetting that a Bichon Frise was on my Bucket List.

Hitchhikers

When we got back to Hell Paradiso after our visit to The Resort, my old man took Boo and Sully to the dog station while I rustled up some frozen burritos and chips. When they returned from the walk, both dogs were scratching like crazy, and my old man looked like his head was about to explode.

"That filthy pit smelled so bad and was so full of crap, I couldn't stand it." he fumed. "From now on, Sully and Boo can shit in the middle of the road, and I don't give a fuck what management has to say about it."

I had rarely seen my old man so thoroughly agitated and using such vulgar language. I handed him a burrito and a cold beer in the hopes of settling him down. We were leaving for Oceanview at the end of the week, and there was no reason for a profanity-laced rant about conditions in the park at this late date.

Sully and Boo hopped onto the couch, and Sully buried his muzzle in his crotch and scratched furiously at his ear with one leg. Boo was also busily scratching and biting at her back and belly. I sat down between them and ruffled Boo's fur. I leapt up in panic-stricken horror.

"What the motherfucking, cocksucking, mothershit-fuck is this?" I bellowed. "They're covered with fucking, sucking shitfuck fleas from that fucking cockshit dog station!"

We put aside our half-eaten burritos and sprang into action. My old man turned on the water heater and moved the wine boxes out of the tiny shower tub while I gathered towels, rags, flea soap and spray. When the water was warm, I filled the tub and plunked Boo and Sully in it.

I knelt in the cramped space and lathered them up to their necks and the backs of their ears, letting the poisonous insecticides work their deadly magic on the fleas, and probably on myself and the dogs.

I lathered their heads with baby shampoo, and after scrubbing them vigorously with an old dish washing brush, rinsed them with the hand-held shower hose. When I was finished, the bottom of the tub was covered with dead fleas.

While I was washing the dogs, my old man rounded up all of our bedding, dog blankets, etc., and took them over to the park's laundry room, where he emptied all the change makers of their quarters and commandeered 6 heavy-duty washers.

After I dried off Sully and Boo, I sprayed them and the couch and floor with more flea spray. I knew what we were in for. Boo settled down and stopped scratching, but Sully, who was deathly allergic to fleas - even if one just hopped on him for a second - was still itchy and had patches of red, mottled skin on his undercarriage and his legs. Having had previous experience with his severe allergic reaction, I had brought along a remedy in the form of organic coconut oil.

I had also purchased a bottle of pure, organic neem oil, which was said to increase the potency of the coconut oil when added in proportional amounts. I melted the congealed coconut oil, along with chunks of neem in the microwave.

With Sully resting comfortably on a towel, I dipped my hands into the warm goo and began massaging it into his tummy and sides.

He rolled onto his back and groaned with relief as the healing properties of the herbal mixture began to soothe his irritated skin. After a minute or two he fell asleep, and I started to notice a sort of unpleasant, sulfurous odor emanating from him.

My old man, back from the laundry with an armful of clean blankets, sniffed the air and made his Mr. Yuk face. "It smells like Satan farted in here," he observed. I had to admit it *was* rank. I frowned and sniffed around the couch.

"I think it's coming from Sully," I said. "I put some coconut and neem oil on him, and I think it's causing him to fart in his sleep."

"Well, whatever's causing it, he doesn't smell like a pina colada like the last time you used that coconut stuff on him." My old man put down the blankets and continued to snuffle around the trailer like a pig rooting for truffles.

"God's teeth," he exclaimed, "The farty smell is coming from *you*!"

I raised my hand, thinking I might very well strike him for the insult and the hoity-toity Elizabethan profanity, when a whiff of acrid nastiness assaulted my senses. It was my hands – the same hands I'd just used to slather the coconut-neem mixture on Sully.

"Holy crap, it must be the neem oil. It's even overpowering the coconutty smell!"

"Go wash that stuff off and spray some Lysol on your hands," he ordered. "It's making me gag." I knew then my old man was serious, because I'd seen him wolf down a tuna sandwich after only a half-box of wine.

"But what about Sully – he stinks to high heaven."

"Not my problem," the disrespectful, foul-mouthed old turd replied, "He's sleeping in *your* bunk tonight."

The next day, a Monday, Sully and Boo were much improved, and there were no more signs of fleas on either one of them. To make sure, I'd be using a fine-tooth flea comb on them twice a day to stop any new hitchhikers in their tracks.

And we wouldn't be taking them anywhere near the filthy, parasite-ridden dog stations either. I'd let them shit on our neighbors' doorstep or in the street as my old man had rudely suggested. If the intrusive, drunken hag who was taking a shortcut through our site every day stepped in their crap, well, *fuck her*.

I was sick of always being Ms. Nice Guy to villaggio idiots. And anyways, we were leaving this fleabag trailer park and heading back to Oceanview, our *real* home and true paradiso, at the end of the week. I had even started packing up some of my better Tupperware pieces in anticipation.

THE MORAL OF THIS STORY

Refer to Chapter 6, **THE MORAL OF THIS STORY**. Like I've said so many times before, I get soooo tired of having to do all the research for you people. If you don't start doing some of the work yourselves, I'm going to charge *a lot more* for my books and put tariffs on other people's books so you won't be able to buy them. And then where will you be?

AUTHOR'S NOTE: Being the experienced editor I am, I went to Chapter 6 to make sure that the MORAL OF THIS STORY applies to this chapter, as indicated above. I'm not sure it does, but I'll be damned if I'm going to do anymore research on your behalf, especially considering how little you paid for this book. If you need a better moral, you'll just have to write it yourself. Enough is enough.

16 - THE FART OF THE DEAL

On Tuesday, the day after Monday and three, possibly 2 ½ days before Friday (if my math is correct) - the day we were going to leave for Oceanview - my old man came home from work looking a little less geezerous than usual.

In fact, his whole demeanor, which was a cross between giddy and slightly fearful, aroused my suspicions. When he said we were going to Del Taco for an Epic Burrito, I knew something heavy was coming down. He didn't spring for fine dining unless he had some kind of earth-shattering news.

"Well, you'll never guess what happened at the office today," he began, picking grains of rice and mashed pinto beans from his bearded garbage hole.

"Did they ask you to keep working and not retire like you were going to tell them and which was the main reason we came back to this shithole?" As was his custom, he appeared not have heard my guess.

"They asked if I'd delay retirement and keep working for them another year or so. A second programmer quit, and the guy who was managing their financial projects got in a wreck and has a bad concussion. He's going to be on medical leave for at least six months, and may not come back at all. I'm the only one left who's experienced with all their systems and applications."

I continued to chew my burrito, letting him go on with his build-up to the finale I'd already figured out. He was going to ask me if I could endure another year in Helltown.

"So, anyway, there'd be a *substantial* increase in salary. Plus, they've offered to rent a nice furnished apartment for us close to the office and pay for storing the travel trailer if we'll stay for another year."

"What about Oceanview?" I asked. "We've done a lot of work on the site and on the trailer. We can't just abandon the place and stay here for a whole year. We didn't even bring all our clothes with us."

"That's the beauty of the deal," he said. They'll give me a $10,000 bonus up front and two weeks of paid vacation so we can go back and hire someone to take care of the lot and trailer for us while we're here."

"We can bring the truck *and* the Prius back with us. They also agreed that we can go back whenever we need a break, and while we're gone, I can telecommute from there just like I've been doing. I didn't give them an answer yet because I wanted to talk it over with you first."

I took another slurp of my soft drink. It wasn't very good. In fact, it smelled kind of like a cat fart. Maybe it was just the scent of neem oil lingering on my fingertips.

I pondered the offer. The extra money *did* sound great, and the furnished apartment…Jesus, it would probably have a shower and a big bath tub, and a 50-gallon water heater and a regular flush toilet – maybe two flush toilets, and a dish washer, and a big screen TV, and covered parking – my mind was spinning with the luxurious possibilities.

My old man wadded up his empty burrito wrapper and looked me in the eye.

"Whatever you decide is ok with me. If you want to stay here another year in an apartment, we can earn a tidy sum before I retire; but if you want to go back to Oceanview and live there for good, that's fine too. Whatever makes you happy."

Where the hell had I heard *that* before?

THE MORAL OF THIS STORY

Never make a deal with, or sell your soul to the Devil. In the end, you won't be happy with the return on your investment.

17 - HOME SICK

We got back to Oceanview toward the end of the following week. The trip itself hadn't been too bad this time. Boo and Sully behaved reasonably well on the long drive, and the RV parks we stayed at, for the most part, were pretty nice.

The flea infestation had been conquered, and Sully's allergic reaction had cleared up. But I was sick, about as sick as I'd ever been, with a pounding headache, high fever and a cough.

Somehow, my old man had avoided the season's rampaging scourge, probably because he'd gotten himself a flu shot – one of those super powerful ones they give geezers. Being decades younger, more resistant to old people diseases, and chronically needle-phobic, I had eschewed the injection, which I felt was not necessary to my well-being.

During our days on the road I'd toughed it out, doped up on Severe Cold & Flu medications and whining pitifully from the passenger seat. At night I slept fitfully, if at all, propped up against the trailer's slide-out wall, trying to breathe through lungs full of Brillo pads.

I began to fear I actually might die, pissing my pants as Ratso Rizzo had at the end of *Midnight Cowboy,* sitting next to Jon Voight on a Greyhound Bus on the way to Florida.

I sympathized with the hapless Ratso, for if I had to sit next to that prick Jon Voight on a Greyhound Bus all the way to Florida, I'd probably piss my pants and die too. This was different, though. It was *me* pissing my pants and dying, not Dustin Hoffman.

At Oceanview, everything was locked up and as we'd left it. My old man had rigged a chain barrier across the front of our lot, mainly to keep Stan Carlyle and his ilk from using it as a parking lot while we were away.

The yard was kind of weedy, and pine needles had collected on the roof of the trailer and the new deck, but it wasn't anything my old man, armed with a step ladder, a long-handled broom and a flu shot couldn't take care of.

After he backed the travel trailer into its parking space, I left everything in it, went inside the big trailer, and collapsed on the bed. I was still feeling terrible, to the extent I could barely keep down a box of wine.

I partly recovered over the next few days, at least enough to unpack some of our stuff. The wheezy cough was still there, though, and I had almost zero energy.

Boo and Sully, sensing my feverish distress and breathing problems, sympathetically limited their demands to thrice-a-day feedings and poop walks, grooming, treats, massages, and constant attention.

The weather got rainier and colder, and I still couldn't seem to shake the flu. At night, the congestion worsened considerably. I coughed and cleared my throat constantly, and had trouble breathing. I kept the window beside the bed open, just to take in enough oxygen. Then I'd get cold in the middle of the night and have to close it.

The wheezing was worse than ever, and my old man finally took Boo and Sully, and started sleeping on the pull-out couch in the living area. At least the three of them could get some rest whilst I was noisily dying in the other room.

In the mornings when I got up, my eyes were nearly swollen shut, and I didn't start feeling better until midday. Then, after I went to bed at night, the symptoms ratcheted up. I was beginning to think I had walking pneumonia. Or maybe just plain old fucking pneumonia. Whichever kind of pneumonia I had, it was wearing me down to the bone.

Since we didn't have a doctor lined up at Oceanview, I was on the verge of hitting the nearest ER and risking a shot of antibiotics, when one morning I chanced to pull our new foam mattress out from the wall in the course of rotating it end to end. What I found explained my lingering upper respiratory problems.

The back edge of the mattress cover was up against the wall, and the area directly under where my pillow rested was stained a blackish purple. The nasty stain had permeated the cover and invaded the mattress itself. There was no question. It was mold, and the spores were what was killing me.

With my old man helping, we dragged the disgusting giant sponge from the trailer, and he hauled it to the dump, along with our pillows. I replaced all of the bedding with non-allergic pillows and a comforter, along with allergen-proof covers. Then I ordered a new mattress from Amazon and washed all our sheets in hot water laced with disinfectant.

When my old man checked behind the bed after the mattress was out, he immediately saw the culprit: a leak along the top edge of the slide-out had caused the wall to get wet while we were gone.

The dampness had wicked into the foam of the mattress, creating a perfect environment for mold. While we were waiting for the new mattress to arrive, we washed down the walls with more disinfectant and ran a HEPA air purifier with UV.

My old man climbed onto the roof of the trailer and re-caulked everything in sight, after which he built a "roof" system with leftover plastic panels from the deck project. The roof would protect the slide-outs from rain in the future. Two days later the new foam mattress came, and immediately thereafter my health started to improve dramatically, and the wheezing disappeared.

I'd taken a major risk and almost sacrificed my life when my old man claimed that he would do *whatever made me happy* – stay put in Helltown, or return to Oceanview. I had lied and told him it would make me happy if he accepted his employer's offer and we stayed put. As I expected, he turned down the offer and we'd returned to Oceanview - for good. It's called *"reverse psychology,"* folks.

THE MORAL OF THIS STORY

Once in a blue moon shit actually works out for the best, even for us Trailer Dogs. After we'd been back at Oceanview for two weeks, my old man's employer called and made him an *even better* offer than before.

If he worked for them for another year – at a *very* high hourly rate - he could continue to telecommute from Oceanview, choose his own hours, and participate in whatever projects he wanted to work on.

Plus, they'd continue to match contributions to his 401K. Naturally, he accepted, and it dramatically increased our retirement funds and more than covered our living expenses at Oceanview.

Now I could relax in the sun, which had returned along with milder temperatures, blooming flowers, and gentle seaside breezes. Best of all, my old man's telecommuting kept us in primo weed, and he was out of my hair for most of the day. And that, dear reader, made me *really fucking happy.*

18 - DONALD J. TRUMP VS MY MOM

If you're reading the third installment of *Trailer Dogs*, which I suspect you are, you're ***not*** a "Trump person." And if you *do* consider yourself a "Trump person," boy howdy, you sure as hell came to the wrong place, sister. Get out now before your head explodes and your brain trickles out of your ass.

The only good thing I have to say about the current President of the United States is

Well, try as I might, I can't think of anything. Sorry about that. LeBron James spoke for me, and a whole lot of other people when he started a tweet to Trump with the words "U bum." So succinct - so crisp - so totally accurate was that expression, it convinced me LeBron has a future as a best-selling author ahead of him when he retires from basketball.

Maybe by the time *Trailer Dogs 3* is published, Trump will have resigned, been impeached and thrown out of office, or serving time in Federal prison. Any or all of the three would be fine with me.

Me and my old man both voted for Hillary, and we firmly believe she won. And the way Trump goes into convulsions at the mere suggestion of Russian interference in the outcome of the election, I have a feeling the orange shitgibbon believes it too.

By whatever means Trump is eventually driven from office, the damage he's done to our democracy, with help from GOP members of Congress and sadly, a few gutless Democrats, is going to last for years to come. America's become the laughing stock of the world, thanks to his bumbling incompetence and (so far) unpunished criminality.

Like an ant queen suddenly unearthed from her chamber, the Trump Administration lies exposed to the sun, while her confused attendants scramble around in their tunnels trying to save the doomed and bloated queen. Sorry guys, the old queen's done laid one too many eggs. Her days on the throne are numbered.

How could this have happened to us? America used to be so compassionate, so welcoming, and so morally superior in every way.

I mean, it sort of says that right there on our Statue of Liberty, doesn't it? "Give me your tired, your poor, your huddled masses yearning to be free." Nowadays, Trump's trying to figure out a way to pay for a big fucking wall to keep people out. We may have to have to change Lady Liberty's meme to:

"Give me your billionaires and your Russians, and shove your huddled masses up your asses."

Anyways, I guess there's no sense in crying over spilt milk, as they say, except for the Russians are already prepping for our next elections, and their man in the White House and his servants in Congress **don't. give. a. shit**. That may be because they've been in on the scam from the git-go.

The Tax Cut For Billionaires was what they wanted, and they got it. The rest of us got screwed. Believe it. When the cost of living starts rising (and it already has), and Walmart is the only place someone in the middle class can get healthcare, Trumpers will have Trump and the GOP to thank for it. But see, *they won't do that*. What they will do on their impoverished sickbeds is: *Blame Democrats*.

My mother's been gone for decades, and I'm grateful she didn't live to see this terrible erosion of America's democracy. I've written about Mom in TD 1 and 2. She was a solid Roosevelt Democrat, widowed when I was only five years old and my dad died suddenly of heart failure.

My dad hadn't been able get life insurance because of Type 1 diabetes and his up-all-night-gambling habit, and Mom was left with a mortgage on a small house, four or five very down-scale properties from Dad's real estate company (his shifty business partner had claimed the best ones for himself), and a five year old daughter to raise. My three older sisters and brother were married and on their own.

Days after he died, thuggish men showed up at our front door to collect Dad's gambling losses. They could tell right away Mom was grief-stricken and didn't have the means to cover the debts, and they left us alone. But the fear they'd come back was always there.

Mom was a devout Christian and never once wavered in her belief that "the Lord would provide." She, in fact, was a provider. Her kindnesses and charity were legendary. Mom fed every stray dog and cat in the neighborhood, and her generosity extended to neighborhood kids as well.

She worried that our paperboy's coat wasn't warm enough, so she went out and bought him a new jacket. She gave it to him under the pretext that it belonged to my brother and didn't fit him anymore.

When he came to collect for the paper on Saturdays, she invited him in and fed him lunch because she thought he looked skinny and undernourished. She always gave him a big tip and a few cookies to take with him when he left to finish his route.

Everybody loved Mom, especially my friends. When I was in high school, many times I'd come home from the mall or a movie, and one or another of my girlfriends would be sitting in the living room, having spent the whole evening with Mom, eating snacks and listening to her stories about growing up poor, and as the eldest of 14, the family babysitter.

Most of my friends came from fairly well-off families – at least compared to mine – and it always struck me as weird that they'd rather spend a Friday or Saturday night at our tiny house than in their parents' air-conditioned, 5-bedroom Colonials. Thinking back, Mom must have given them attention and love they weren't getting at home.

Although our town was extremely segregated at the time and racism was at its height, Mom was color blind. After my dad died, she found out right away that the rundown houses in rundown neighborhoods weren't going to be enough to support us.

Most of the properties had been rented or sold on contract to deadbeats who never paid on time, or who skipped town owing months of back rent. Mom didn't have it in her to track them down, mainly because she felt badly about them having made any payments on the houses in the first place.

She got a job waitressing, and then enlisted my sisters and brother to help fix up the houses. They spent hours and hours at those places, mowing grass, cutting weeds, repairing walls and roofs, and painting. When they were finally presentable, she placed ads in the local newspaper.

The first couple who called about one of the houses had driven by it on their way home from church, and had stopped to peek through the windows.

They apparently liked what they saw, because as soon as they got home they called Mom and asked if they could come by and talk to her. They were interested not in renting the house, but possibly buying it on contract. Mom gave them our address and directions, and told them to drop by later that day.

When a car pulled up in our driveway, a black couple got out. A young boy and girl emerged from the back seat, and they all walked up to our door.

Their last name was Howard, and Mr. Howard worked at the Post Office as a letter carrier, and Mrs. Howard cleaned houses to supplement their income. Mom immediately invited them to stay for dinner, but they politely declined, although they did accept her offer of coffee and homemade oatmeal cookies.

While the adults chatted, I took the boy (I remember him as tall and nerdy, with thick glasses) and girl to my room to show them my toys and box games. They sat stiffly on the edge of my bed in their Sunday clothes, looking a little nervous and not saying much.

The girl was tiny and cute, and wore her hair in two frizzy buns at the sides of her head. I immediately wanted Mom to fix my hair like that because I thought she looked like a bear cub, and I wanted to look like a bear cub too. Unfortunately, my hair was long, white-blonde, and I looked more like Cindy Brady.

Mom gave the Howards the keys to the house and told them to go back and look at it inside and out. If they were still interested they could call back the next day.

I know how unbelievable Mom's trust in complete strangers sounds today, but back then few people ran credit checks, and folks in our small town were more likely to trust you if you dressed up for church on Sunday, had good manners and well-behaved children.

Mom had two out of three of those prerequisites herself, and she instinctively trusted the Howards because they were three for three.

It didn't matter to her that they were African-American, and it wouldn't have mattered if they were Mexican-American or Asian-American or even Canadian-American. But I'll be totally honest here and admit that, had they been Russians, a *recognized* adversary of the United States, it *would have* mattered. Mom, as kind-hearted as she was, wouldn't have handed Russians the key to our front door.

The Howards ended up buying the house on contract, and when they first moved in, redneck white folks who lived in the neighborhood, and who kept rusting cars and engine parts and broken swing sets in their own weedy front yards, had fits. The Howards had to deal with name-calling, threats, and garbage dumped over their fence – in the daytime and at night.

Even *our* neighbors, some of whom were even lower on the social stratum than we were, felt compelled to comment at the "impropriety" of a "colored man" entering their neighborhood when Mr. Howard came to our house once a month to make a payment. And, for God's sake, what was a black man doing going into a *white* widow's house - for whatever reason? It was scandalous.

But neither the Howards nor my mom budged an inch. They fixed up their small house, and eventually added a third bedroom and built a garage. They were never late with a payment. We exchanged Christmas cards with them, and Mom always had small gifts for their kids when they came in December.

When Mom died, the Howards were in their late 60's. Mr. Howard had retired from the Post Office, and they'd paid off the house years before.

The whole Howard family came to her funeral, including the nerdy son, who was married and had a baby daughter, and his sister, who was in college. Their presence attracted little attention at that time, because they weren't the only black faces among the mourners. And they certainly weren't the only of my mother's friends in tears.

Mom was Baptist (later Methodist), but she didn't discriminate against people of different faiths. Well, maybe just a little. She didn't like the Jehovah's Witnesses who came to our door and interrupted her reading, but that didn't stop her from inviting them in for a glass of iced tea and snacks.

Mom *loved* the Mormon missionaries who came around occasionally, but that was mostly because they were exceedingly polite and wore short-sleeve white shirts and ties, and she was a sucker for good grooming.

After they'd stated their case and left, she'd shake her head and say "Those Mormons have a lot of wives." Fearing that she might have gone too far in her criticism, she'd add "But I hear they treat them very well."

Of Catholics, she worried about their supplications to saints, which she considered the worship of false idols. "I don't think Pastor Clark would approve of that," she noted. "It's the road to perdition."

But any time Bishop (later Archbishop) Fulton J. Sheen, the Catholickest of Catholics, was on TV, Mom was spellbound by him. As of this writing, Archbishop Sheen's canonization is still up for grabs, but I'm convinced Mom would vote YES if she had a say in the matter.

I had Jewish friends in grade school and in high school. Our neighborhood was on the other side of the highway from theirs, and for the most part, they were the children of retail store owners and lawyers.

Call it stereotyping if you will, but Mom believed that Jews were innately smarter than Christians, despite their rejection of her Lord and Savior. "It's not up to us to judge or punish them for not believing in Jesus," she told me, "and they've suffered more than enough with concentration camps and Hitler."

I spent a lot of time at my friend Rachel's house. Rachel was Jewish and played the cello, and we were both in the school's orchestra. I'd hitch a ride with her to early practice twice a week, sometimes spending the night.

As a young woman, Rachel's grandmother, who lived with Rachel's family, had spent time in a concentration camp. She had a faint number tattooed on the underside of her arm, and she showed it to me one day. She never talked about her experience and neither did Rachel.

I knew practically nothing about the Holocaust, because for whatever reason, it had been largely passed over at my school. I began reading about it, and was horrified beyond imagination.

After that, I could barely look Nana in the eye without feeling tremendous shame over her suffering like that. I *do* remember, as Rachel and I were primping for school one morning, Nana came to the bathroom door and looked us both over as we stood scrunched together in front of the mirror.

"Girls," she said in a heavy German accent, "Always groom your eyebrows first. Your face will follow." We waited until she'd walked down the hall to break into hysterics.

Mom didn't discriminate against gays and Lesbians either. Back then, we were in the dark about bisexuals and transgenders, and didn't know they existed. The topic of one's sexuality wasn't discussed, and maybe with good reason in our family. One of Mom's younger brothers was a closeted, but *notably* gay man, as were two of my cousins.

There were also Lesbians or two or three in Mom's circle of family and friends as I later learned, but she honestly thought they were "old maids," and had never found husbands to their liking. I suppose in a way she was right about that. Her Aunt Edna, a school teacher, was one, and Mom absolutely adored Edna and her "best friend," Katherine, who lived with Edna their whole lives.

Mom, naïve and completely bereft of "gaydar," went to her grave thinking she might have a shot with Rock Hudson.

She was also a huge fan of Liberace, and when he was in town for a performance, you would find her somewhere in the crowd. "I don't think people should make fun of Liberace just because he likes fancy clothes," Mom said. "Those are his costumes, and he doesn't dress like that every day. He's a brilliant musician and a wonderful son to his mother."

Mom was fond of Elvis Presley too, and for many of the same reasons, but she didn't approve of his suggestive gyrations on-stage.

On the other hand, there was the pink Cadillac Elvis bought for his mother, Gladys, so his pelvic thrusts and wild movements were forgivable in her eyes. When he married Pricilla after his service in the U.S. Army, Mom was convinced The King had settled down for good.

Now, I'm not saying that my mom was a saint, because she wasn't, although she did work the occasional miracle. Like the time Uncle Boots got drunk at Thanksgiving dinner and started loudly berating Aunt Dorothy.

With a smile on her face and napkin in her hand, Mom said "Shut your goddamn mouth, Boots." And he *did* for about five minutes, mostly because he was so shocked to hear her use the Lord's name in vain. But his silence, however brief, was no less a miracle as far as we were all concerned.

Anyways, as I said, Mom didn't believe in sainthood, for herself or anyone else, even though she didn't hold it against the Catholics.

She was Irish and had a quick temper, but Mom cooled down fast and never held a grudge. When I got out of control as I sometimes did, I could count on *The Wrath of The Clamp*. The Clamp was the forefingers and thumb of Mom's right hand, which would clamp down on either side of my mouth until I looked (and felt) like a catfish on the hook.

If The Clamp moved forward or backwards, I moved right along with it. It was probably a lot like a stuffed toy feels in the grasp of a claw machine, if the stuffed toy is a snot-nose, smart-ass kid and the claw is her Mom's vice-like hand.

While in the grasp of The Clamp, Mom familiarized me with the behavioral transgression for which I was being clamped. More often than not it was my saying something she thought irreverent or blasphemous.

Mom was always concerned with the state of my immortal soul, and she worried that at the rate I was going I wouldn't make it into Heaven, where she, my brother and sisters, and hopefully my dad, would be waiting for me one day.

She had no idea that *she* was the one responsible for planting seeds of doubt and eventual atheism in me when I asked her if dogs and cats went to heaven.

"No," she said authoritatively. "Dogs and cats and other pets have Heavens of their own. Our Heaven is all people." That pretty much did it for me. No way did I want any part of a place that discriminated against dogs and cats. Birds, snakes and hamsters could fend for themselves, however.

My mother wasn't a feminist, per se, but she almost always took the side of other women in any dispute, sometimes even if they didn't deserve it. She was more comfortable around women, which I believe was a combination of having been raised with a verbally abusive, alcoholic father, and being drop-dead beautiful, which made her a target for every skirt-chasing male in town from the time she was 14 years old.

She was well-read and extraordinarily artistic, and in another time and place she might have been a successful artist.

Her own mother, overwhelmed with caring for fourteen children, delegated a lot of responsibility to Mom at an early age, although grandma somehow found the time to teach her how to sew, crochet, knit, draw and paint.

Behind Mom's perfect cheekbones, green eyes and strawberry blonde façade, beat the heart of an extremely shy person, forced into taking charge when she was widowed relatively young.

Wham Bam, Sorry Sam

Mom was strong, but sometimes it got to be too much for her. I remember when we'd go to town on some Friday afternoons when she got off work, and she'd hand me her paperwork and checks, and tell me to take them down to the savings & loan, which was staffed by six middle aged women.

The president of the bank was Mrs. Walker, who'd known Mom and Dad for years, and who'd handled all my dad's real estate transactions. Mom would wait for me at the corner, she said, because she had "something I want to look at in the lingerie shop," and besides, Mrs. Walker and the other ladies at the bank "...always get such a kick out of talking to you."

I would trot down to the bank armed with the checks and a hilarious joke to amuse the all-female audience. I loved my gigs at the bank, not only for the yuks my jokes got, but for the water cooler in Mrs. Walker's private office, which fascinated and delighted me beyond all reason.

It was an old-fashioned cooler, with a big upside down glass jar and a metal bracket that held pointy paper cups. The water was always cold, and I drank cup after cup of it, and watched with something akin to rapture of the deep as big bubbles blurped to the top of the jar, which was actually the bottom, what with it being upside down and all.

The routine I performed for my admirers at the bank usually consisted of riddles I had memorized, such as "What's black & white and red all over? (newspaper), or the latest (Forgive me, Mr. President) moron joke: Why did the moron tiptoe past the medicine cabinet? (so he wouldn't wake up the sleeping pills) (Forgive me, Melania). I never failed to get applause, and sometimes a candy bar for my efforts.

The only time my performance went awry was the afternoon I told a joke I'd overheard my brother-in-law tell to my brother.

It was about an old bull instructing his son about love-making. The father bull tells his son to run down to the pasture, mount every cow he sees, and when he's finished, to politely say: 'Wham, bam, thank you, ma'am.' The son does what his father told him, but when he's finished with the last cow, he says, 'Wham, bam - sorry Sam!'

I was about seven at the time, and had absolutely no idea what the joke meant, only that I liked the rhyming in it, and my brother had roared with laughter when he heard it. Not so with the ladies at the bank, who rolled their eyes and looked at each other with tight smiles.

Mom was waiting for me at the corner, and I told her about the unappreciative audience and how they hadn't laughed at my wham-bam joke. Fortunately, Mom was more attuned to that brand of humor, because she bent over double, laughing, and had to use the restroom in the lingerie shop to keep from pissing herself. (The apple doesn't fall far from the tree, does it?)

Much later, my sister told me that Mom had been terrified to go the bank herself, because Mrs. Walker always lectured her about not being tough enough with tenants who were behind in their rent payments.

Mom wasn't inclined to evict; Mrs. Walker *was*, and Mom couldn't bear the scolding she knew she was in for. After the wham-bam incident, I still went to the bank for her, but she previewed my act before I skipped off with the checks and passbooks.

There were three things my mother taught me to NEVER EVER ask a person:

How much money do you make?

What church do you go to?

Who did you vote for?

On that last one, my Mom's "politics" were fairly simple: She was a Democrat and a Liberal. She respected, but did not "Like Ike." She adored JFK and appreciated LBJ's social reforms, but not his war in Vietnam. She thought the world of Jimmy Carter, but was influenced more by his resemblance to my Uncle Ernie, both in looks and temperament. She could not abide Nixon.

The politician Mom most admired was Shirley Chisholm, the first black woman elected to Congress. Chisholm represented the 12th Congressional District in New York, serving seven terms.

Nobody in my family was ever really certain what it was about Shirley Chisholm that so captivated Mom, especially since none of us had ever been anywhere near New York. But whatever it was, it was strong. At every family gathering she could be counted to go on and on about Shirley Chiz-Home as Mom called her, until we all wanted to tear our hair out.

In 1972 Chisholm ran for the Democratic nomination, and Mom was beside herself with joy. She told everybody who'd listen that she thought Shirley Chiz-Home could and should be the next President of the United States, and Mom was certain she could beat the vile and contemptible Nixon, whom everyone knew was a liar and a crook.

It was not to be, however, and George McGovern secured the nomination that year. Mom had nothing against McGovern, and in fact supported his call for an immediate end to the War in Vietnam. He just wasn't her first choice for the Democrats' candidate.

Always optimistic, Mom said she believed that one day America would have an African American president, but it probably wouldn't be a woman, because Americans seemed to hate women even more than they hated African American men. She didn't live to see Obama elected or Hillary Clinton lose to Donald Trump, or realize that she was correct on both counts.

THE MORAL OF THIS STORY

My mother was a kind, compassionate Christian, with high moral standards and a generous soul. Trump is a phony Christian and a callous man, with no moral compass. Mom would have detested him, just as I do. When it comes to a comparison between POTUS and my mom, nolo contendere.

The following is a poem I wrote for her many years ago:

My Mother's Paper Shoes

A raw winter day
Around 1917 or thereabouts,
Her cheek and two small handprints
Kissed the frosty window
Of the Canal Street Department Store.
She stared, wide-eyed and hopeful,
At the most beautiful shoes she'd ever seen
Perfectly buckled, perfectly heeled, perfectly new
Perfectly unobtainable
By a girl who shared a bed,
Often wet
A meal,
Never enough
With thirteen others
Whose shoes were never new
Humming a silly song,
And sitting on cracked linoleum
In the family "parlor"
Beside peeling cabbage roses
In front of a coal oil stove,
She put crayon stub to newsprint.
Using her own foot for a pattern,
And in her childish hand,
She drew her new shoes
Even more beautiful
Even more perfect
Than the shoes in the window
Of the Canal Street Department Store.
Red instead of brown,
With bows instead of buckles,
And across their newsprint soles,
Doughboys, marching off to war.
Sitting on cracked linoleum
In the family "parlor"
Beside peeling cabbage roses
In front of a coal oil stove,
She began to cut them out,
When it came to her they were not real
Like her father's drunken rages
Like her mother's weary sighs
Like ghostly soldiers marching off to war
On the soles
Of my mother's paper shoes

Mom's drawings

Mom, probably in her early 30's

19 - ODDS & ENDINGS

After he read *Trailer Dogs 2*, my old man said it could have used "a few more yuks." I should advise you that he also thinks Adam Sandler is "sort of funny at times," so you can't entirely trust his opinion on these matters.

Because of his smoldering jealousy of me, he is now working on his own book as he puts it, "to set the record straight." If that's still not enough to convince you of his rapidly diminishing brain cells, he recently took up the guitar because, knee-deep into his twilight years, he wants to "...learn to play just like Eric Clapton."

Well, hell, now I've lost my train of thought.

Oh yeah, now I remember. My old man claims I need to wrap up some more loose ends in *Trailer Dogs 3*. He pointed to a number of subjects he feels need further comment. So, in deference to the very small percentage of readers who probably agree with this dumb assessment, here goes.

AUTHOR'S NOTE: So far, my old man's mastered "My Dog Has Fleas" on the guitar. I don't think he realizes it's a mnemonic device for tuning ukuleles. Anyways...

Recipes

I had forgotten all about my promise to include more recipes in *Trailer Dogs 3*. Actually, I don't think I ever promised to include more recipes in *Trailer Dogs 3*.

In fact, I'm absolutely certain no promises were made *by me* concerning recipes of any kind, so there's no need for you to go back in the book and check for yourself. As we've already established, you're too lazy to do shit for yourselves, so take my word on it.

As you may know, I'm currently writing an important book about current events, so I don't have time to sit down with anyone, let alone you, to discuss whether a promise was made or not made, concerning recipes.

In fact, now that I've given the subject even more consideration, I believe the false suggestion - that I promised more recipes – may have been leaked by my old man in an attempt to besmirch my good name and reputation with readers.

As soon as *Trailer Dogs 3* is published, I'll track down the leak and sue whoever was responsible for it. I will want a really smart lawyer, one who will work for free. Obviously, it will have to be a Jew, so it's going to be hard to find that combo, if you take my meaning.

Trailer Dogs, The Movie

As readers know, I had very high hopes for making *Trailer Dogs* – both 1 and 2 - into movies. Sadly, my exertions have come to naught (zero, nothing, nix, zilch, goose egg, not anything) - for those of you who don't have access to a Thesaurus (a book that lists words in groups of synonyms and related concepts) or a Dictionary (a book with definitions of shit in it).

Regardless of all that, and despite my best efforts, I was unable to gain the attention of certain well-known Hollywood producers (Mr. Harvey Weinstein for one), celebrities and film stars, many of whom have been, for whatever reason, too caught up in their own sordid affairs and lawsuits to even return my calls or respond to my letters.

Kevin Spacey is but one example. I attempted to contact Spacey through his agent time and time again, with little response other than threats to take legal action unless I "ceased and desisted" in what the agent termed "harassment."

My emails could not be construed as harassment in any sense of the word. I merely wanted Mr. Spacey to agree to portray my old man in the *Trailer Dogs* movies, and if the role required sexual contact between Mr. Spacey and me, Mr. Spacey would be forced to comply by the terms of our contract and my position as the film's Executive Producer.

When Spacey proved to be uncooperative, it was suggested to me by a friend that I should try contacting Bill Cosby, who would be perfect in the part of my old man due to his horrific looks and corny, yet truly obnoxious comedic talent.

I discarded the idea on the grounds that Cosby is too decrepit and too repugnant to portray even my old man, and in addition to that, he is well-known for his aversion to performing profane and off-color humor, which are hallmarks of *Trailer Dogs 1-3*.

However, not wanting to invite any suggestion of racism on my part in the matter as it pertained to a black man, I contacted the agents of Denzel Washington, Will Smith, Jamie Foxx, and Blair Underwood to offer them the role.

I never heard back from any of them. I can only surmise it was due either to their unwillingness to work with a white actress, or their hesitance to perform certain acts of a sexual nature required by my screenplay.

In essence, and because of the discrimination against me, I have given up on making Trailer Dogs into a movie, or even a cartoon. I hope these people are happy. Their gain is my loss or some such shit.

Walmart

My battles with the retail giant continue, so to speak. I rarely buy anything there anymore since they caught onto customers getting a good deal on their $49 a year delivery fee and cancelled it. If there's one thing the Walton family won't stand for it's their customers getting a good deal. Seriously.

When the Chinese or Vietnamese or whatever sweatshops were manufacturing their clothing line didn't supply the garments cheaply enough, Walmart apparently stopped carrying their brands and started carrying other brands of even more cheaply made clothes.

Unfortunately, for Walmart customers, the new manufacturers were also forced to cut corners, and they drastically reduced the fabric content in the clothes they were now supplying.

Nowadays, when you buy a shirt or pair of pants at Walmart, the ratio of thin air to fabric is approximately 20:1. This is particularly true of the fabrics used in women's panties, which is so lightweight these days it can barely contain a mild fart, let alone a 52" waist. I, for one, find this practice degrading and extraordinarily uncomfortable.

I had thought my bringing this matter to the attention of the Walton family would shame them into putting a stop to it. I was wrong.

At the same time the discount retailer is using air instead of fibers to clothe middle class Americans, it has also raised the price on items that elderly people need to survive. The following is a list of 30 items now too-expensive-to-afford, compiled during my geezer interviews and research:

1. Box wine (Pinot Noir in particular)

2. XXL women's panties

3. Sinus medications

4. Hemorrhoid salve

5. Pork rinds

6. Anti-Diarrhea medication

7. Frozen burritos

8. Laxatives/stool softeners

9. Eye drops

10. Nose drops

11. Ear drops

12. Cough drops

13. Odor Eater Shoe inserts

14. Ingrown toenail remedies

15. Toenail fungus remedies

16. "General" fungus remedies

17. Probiotics

18. Lidocaine patches, creams, sprays

19. Adult diapers

20. Fried pies

21. Acid reducers

22. Depilatory creams/Unwanted hair removal devices

23. Scalp restoration/hair regrowth products

24. Massage/vibrating devices

25. Double and Triple A Batteries

26. Hearing aid batteries

27. Age spot fading creams

28. Plus-size bras

29. Chips (all varieties)

30. Plus-size yoga pants

THE MORAL OF THIS STORY

It is incumbent upon those of those of us in the younger generations to make certain our elders receive the respect and deep discounts they so richly deserve from Walmart, and all retailers for that matter.

I have done my part in bringing these injustices to the attention of the Walmart family, and now it is time for other young people to do the same. I suggest you purchase paperback copies of all three *Trailer Dogs* books for your friends and relatives' Christmas gifts, thus helping to fund my continued advocacy for the elderly.

God Bless.

My tweet to Walmart and their reply:

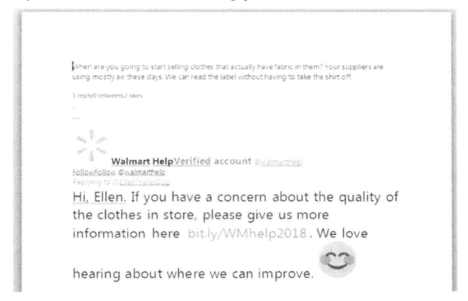

When are you going to start selling clothes that actually have fabric in them? Your suppliers are using mostly air these days. We can read the label without having to take the shirt off.

1 reply 0 retweets 2 likes

Walmart Help Verified account @walmarthelp

FollowFollow @walmarthelp

Replying to @EllenTrailerDog

Hi, Ellen. If you have a concern about the quality of the clothes in store, please give us more information here bit.ly/WMhelp2018 . We love

hearing about where we can improve.

Heh.

20 - LIVING SMALL: RETIREMENT, GEEZER STYLE

Projects on the trailer and in our yard are done, and it's all really terrific, except for my old man's work/hobby shed. I ventured inside the other day, and it looks like a bull elephant fucked a rhino in there, to coin a phrase.

If you've ever seen *District 9*, the sci-fi film about aliens who look like jumbo shrimps, and who are quarantined in a government ghetto camp, my old man organizes his personal spaces exactly like those prawn creatures.

If you haven't seen the film, I've included a few pictures below as examples of my old man's sloppiness. *(NOTE TO TD3 NARRATOR: Feel free to describe what you see here, and don't spare the "holy fucks")*

My old man's side of the closet shelf

My old man's "office"

More of my old man's office décor

My old man's tool shed décor

My old man, napping on the floor after a hard day of watching TV

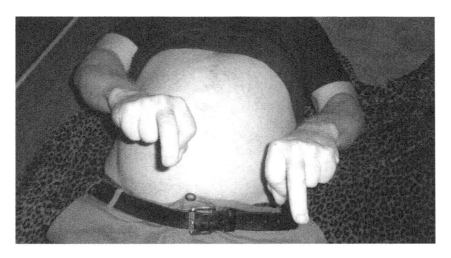

*My old man's rude gesture after realizing I took his
picture while he was napping*

Still, keeping my old man's messes quarantined in sheds and the like is a lot better than him dragging his computer and hobbies *in here*, and yakking and carrying on all day about shit *nobody's* interested in, like sports and video games and TV shows about science.

That sums up what happens when you're married to a disorganized, aging, geezer prawn: Can't live with 'em, and can't find room in the trailer to hide their corpse.

We haven't heard anything from anybody at The Resort since we got back to Oceanview. I wonder how Virginia's doing and if she and "Brownie" have tied the knot yet.

I think about Lonnie and Daisy May once in a while, but only when I see Stan Carlyle hobbling down the street with a scowl on his face, heading over to the clubhouse to take a crap and a shower. I still haven't seen his wife or heard her cane rapping on the wall of their trailer lately.

Lance, Wade, Matt and their Chihuahuas continue to aggravate the crapola out of me, with their shriek-laughter, Popeye song, yip-yapping, and Wade's second-hand cigarette smoke wafting through the shrubbery and into my lungs.

But they *do* take lots of mini vacations in their travel trailer, and they take the dogs with them, so it's not as much of a problem as I thought it would be. Friendships in RV parks are fleeting for some reason, which can be a good thing, if you catch my drift.

My old man is keeping himself busy with computer work and his guitar thing and that book he's writing. I'm not sure, but I think it may be about vampires, like the lady books he's so fond of. He's had some trouble with his guitar lessons, and says his fingers don't work right. I'm thinking it's probably his brain that isn't working right, but don't tell him I said that.

It's almost a century later, and he still whines about how his Mom & evil nuns brow beat him into taking piano lessons, and then smacked him with a wooden ruler when he didn't practice. In a couple weeks he'll be saying the same thing about me, and it will be a lie. I use a bamboo back scratcher.

I found a new friend. If you're a geezer, you probably don't recall my writing about the crazy woman who fostered Boo for the rescue outfit. You can go back to that chapter to refresh your memory, or you can just keep reading and pretend you're not old and lazy and can still remember your own name.

Anyhow, the woman's name is Terry, and I liked to have never got Boo away from her on the day we adopted her.

I was afraid there might be some violence between me and Terry, so I suggested that we cut Boo in half, and Terry could have her butt end. That knocked some sense into her, and she relinquished custody. *(It always pays to do stuff the way they teach you in the Bible.)*

Terry ended up adopting the two Schnauzer girls I'd been tempted to take, and then she went back to foster a pregnant Chihuahua, Chiquita, which she also adopted. She would have adopted Chiquita's three puppies, but her old man put his domineering foot down.

Terry lives in a manufactured home at a trailer park about an hour and a half drive from Oceanview. We kept in touch by email after Boo's adoption and exchanged maybe ten or fifteen billion pictures of our dogs and fifteen billion, give or take a few billion, of other people's dogs.

At Christmas, I sent her a carrying bag for Chiquita, Pork Chomps for all the girls, and a box of chocolates for Terry and her old man. She sent me plush toys for Boo and Sully, liver-flavored treats for the kids, and a box of chocolates for me and my old man.

Terry and I have a lot in common:

- We're married to much older husbands with beards, poor hygiene and exceptionally bad taste in clothing

- We're extremely profane and vulgar, even when it isn't fucking necessary

- We both live in trailer parks

- We prefer similar marijuana strains and varietal box wines

- We're obsessed with dogs

- We love the same TV shows: The Walking Dead, Better Call Saul and Schitt's Creek

- We both enjoy food in substantial quantities, and, coincidentally, wear the same size underwear

- We hate talking on the phone, preferring to email or text, or not speak at all

- We enjoy sharing information about stubborn nasal blockages, bladder control (or lack thereof), bowel movements, sleep habits, musculoskeletal disorders and remedies for therein

We agree on just about everything to one degree or another, such as Adam Sandler not being funny, Dire Straits being the coolest band ever, and things that smell too bad to eat, even if they taste ok once they're in your mouth. It's amazing.

We have discussed most every subject under the sun, with the exception of those Three Deadly Questions my mom told me I should not, under any circumstances ask, and which I reiterate for you below:

How much money do you make?

What church do you go to?

Who did you vote for?

On the church thing, Terry had already told me that she didn't attend, by way of explaining why she was always at the dog park on Sunday mornings. I didn't pursue the topic because, well, frankly I didn't give a shit one way or another.

As to what her family's income was, I didn't care about that either. From what I could tell, she and her old man had enough money to rush their dogs to the vet if their farts smelled "off," and to buy them premium food and treats. And based on Terry's size, they ate pretty well themselves.

Neither of us mentioned anything about politics, although we'd both expressed our outrage at the lack of help Puerto Rico was getting after the hurricane, and once or twice we'd ruminated about how the middle class was getting screwed from all sides.

I didn't know if she was a Democrat, a Republican or an Independent, and honestly, I didn't really want to know. What I *did* know about Terry was that we saw eye to eye on many of the same things, and I hadn't met anyone I'd felt as compatible with in a long, long time.

With our gated deck finished and excellent weather in the forecast, I invited Terry for lunch, and told her to be sure and bring all three dogs with her. Boo was a gentle pushover and Sully was a ladies' man, and I figured they'd all get along fine after the initial pecking order was established and Sully, as the only male, was relegated to the back of the henhouse.

The day of our luncheon I ordered in 40 bucks worth of Chinese food and bought a bag of ice so we could plunk the cubes into our glasses of box wine.

My old man contributed to the party by sweeping the deck and making sure there weren't any floaters in his laundry shed toilet. Then he retired to his work shed, perhaps to work, perhaps to practice his guitar. It was hard to tell based on the sounds coming from it.

When Terry drove up in a black Prius (ours is blue), I immediately noticed she hadn't brought the two Schnauzer girls with her, and I was very disappointed. One of them tended to get carsick, she explained, and she'd left the other at home to keep her sister dog company.

She was transporting Chiquita in the carrier I'd sent at Christmas. The dog was so cute and so irresistible, I regretted not beating Terry to the punch adopting her.

Terry set her down on the deck and we pulled the gates closed. Then I opened the trailer door, and Sully bounced out. Boo stayed inside the trailer, behind the screen door, stretching her neck to catch a glimpse of the seductive stranger.

Sully raced up to Chiquita and began sniffing her from head to tail. The little dog stood stiff and still, staring straight ahead while he conducted his examination. Having found her acceptable, he began to circle around her, playfully nipping at her neck and ears as he did with Boo.

Joining in the game, Chiquita nipped back. The two were having a great time until a shrill, piercing shriek rang out from inside the trailer. It was Boo, and her screeches continued until I had to go in and try to calm her down. She was absolutely furious.

Boo scratched and clawed at me when I picked her up, and her body was tense as she tried to get back to observing her perceived rival through the screen door. Finally, out of desperation, I put her in the bedroom and closed the door. Then I went back out, picked up Sully and brought him inside.

I shut him in the bedroom with Boo, and heard them both jump up on the bed. I figured Sully had a lot of 'splainin' to do.

The rest of the afternoon proceeded much better. Terry went inside the trailer and visited with Sully and his jealous lover, while I fawned over Chiquita on the deck. Damn, she was adorable! I couldn't really blame Sully for the earlier indiscretion.

We ate our Chinese food (my old man helped out) and drank our box wine and exchanged tokens (or I should say tokes) of our favorite cones. Terry had noticed a lot for sale on the way in and was going to take a picture of it on her way out.

Who knew…maybe she and her old man would be our neighbors one of these days. She sat back in the recliner and looked around.

"This is perfection," she said. "You guys really landed in Shangri-La."

Terry was right. Sitting there in the warm breeze, enjoying a dessert of brownies and coffee, I was overcome with happiness. I had pretty decent health, a comfortable home in a safe neighborhood, and a little money in the bank again.

Best of all, I had my dogs and my old man to share it with. And, after losing my lifelong best friend to cancer in 2013, I'd found a new friend, in of all places, a trailer park.

"You know, I voted for Donald Trump," Terry said unexpectedly, breaking my reverie and shocking me to the core.

"We've always voted Republican. I actually thought Trump would be different. I really believed he'd drain the swamp in Washington and bring in a lot more jobs. But he hasn't done a damn thing for anybody but himself and his crooked family. I despise him. And I'll never vote for a Republican again as long as I live."

I inhaled deeply, passed the cone back to Terry, and slowly exhaled.

"Sister, I feel exactly the same way."

THE MORAL OF THE STORY

"If you can't be with the one you love, love the one you're with." – Stephen Stills

EPILOGUE

We made the right choice moving back to the Pacific Northwest. It's been a hell of a lot of work starting over, what with my old man being such a feeb and all, but our persistence seems to have paid off. I wouldn't have thought it possible just a few short years ago when our lives were upside down. Maybe the same thing will be true of America after Trump's gone.

We'll stay put at Oceanview, at least until the cold, wet weather sets in again. When it starts raining, we'll pack up and head south. Maybe to Mexico. I hear they have some pretty good Mexican food there, probably better than Taco Bell if that's possible.

Anyways, it usually starts out gloomy and foggy here in the morning, but the sun eventually comes out, and to quote Chauncey Gardner in the movie *Being There*: "As long as the roots are not severed, all is well. And all will be well in the garden."

Me and my old man have weathered a lot of storms and lived to tell the tale. We're satisfied and content most of the time, and the rest of the time, well, we just try to laugh it off.

At this time I have no plans to write a fourth *Trailer Dogs*, but if interesting things happen during our travels and I can keep my sense of humor long enough to see Trump impeached, maybe I'll change my mind. As Trump himself often says, we'll just have to wait and see.

Until then, we're very grateful for how things have worked out for us, and in most ways, we believe we have triumphed over adversity. And still, we persist.

Thanks, Obama!

EPILOGUE RE-BOOT

Days after I finished the final chapter of *Trailer Dogs 3,* Roseanne Barr's TV show got cancelled when she sent racist tweets that weren't any worse than racist remarks she'd made before, and which were certainly not any worse than the racist tweets she sent after her first racist tweets.

Roseanne initially attempted to defend herself by tweeting that the obnoxious tweet was "a joke." When that excuse fell flat, and a black, female executive at ABC cancelled her show, Roseanne confessed that she'd been stoned on Ambien when she tweeted. But for some reason, she just kept on tweeting more racist shit in addition to jumping the asses of her co-stars.

AUTHOR'S NOTE: The only thing I can figure is that folks on Ambien don't really get any sleep, they just stay up all night tweeting mean, crazy shit. Been there, done that myself, but I have never blamed Ambien for my nocturnal fuck ups. That's because mine are usually the fault of box wine, not prescription drugs.

Anyways, I thought I should come back here to the book and address Barr's name-calling and racist tirades, seeing as how many of my big fat white readers are too lazy and spineless to do it for me.

Let me begin by saying that I like and respect Roseanne as much as Trump likes and respects Jeff Sessions. Folks, if you can't figure out what *that* means, you haven't been paying attention to the disaster that is the Trump Administration, and I can't help you, other than to suggest you order a few hundred copies of *Trailer Dogs* and distribute them to your pals at the asylum.

Many years ago, I knew a woman who was very much like Roseanne, in that she was loud-mouthed and insulting, although she didn't realize she was offensive until the words were out of her mouth. She might have been a close relative of mine for all you know.

"Those pants look like you pissed them and then slept in them," she often said to me, not knowing that she had struck a nerve. Realizing her mistake, she'd add: "Just kidding!"

On another occasion, perhaps during a meal at our house, she might remark to my old man: "Your casserole tastes like a school of dead fish shit in it." Noting his hurt expression, she'd quickly affix "Just kidding" to her tactless (but truthful) observation.

This happened time after time, until me and my old man "normalized" her inexcusable behavior and lack of self-control, and even chuckled at her mindless slights and "just kiddings" as though they were merely the mumblings of an incoherent geezer.

That is until one day, during a visit, she crossed a line that led her spiteful tongue right into oncoming traffic. Our two dogs, Bo and Dolly, a long-bodied toy Poodle, were ripping around the house, chewing the fringe off the rugs and digging Dorito fragments out of the couch - as dogs are wont to do - when Aunt Betty said:

"That Dolly looks more like a wiener dog than a poodle."

We were aghast, and at a loss for words at the gravity of her insult. Finally, registering our barely concealed outrage, she added her customary "Just kidding!"

But it was too late. The damage had been done. Never again was Aunt Betty invited into our home, and her name was forever struck from our list of Christmas card recipients. We ignored her apologies and feeble attempts to mend fences over the years, as we had finally recognized her for what she truly was: a dog hater and an asshole.

The events described above took place a long time ago, when "tweets" were the sounds birds made, and had nothing to do with presidential edicts or ranting racists.

"Aunt Betty," as I have elected to call this anonymous relative, may very well have benefitted had she been able to *tweet* her unthinking and callous remarks. If she were alive today, and I'm not saying she isn't, but if she *were*, she could add an emoji to her vicious tweets instead of "just kidding!"

AUTHOR'S NOTE: For those clueless geezers who don't know what an "emoji" is, it's a smiley face like the ones you used to draw on your niece's birthday card after you stuck a lousy dollar in it.

AUTHOR'S NOTE, CONTINUED: Nowadays, however, the smiley face can have other emotions on it, like a frown, a grimace, a crazy-eyed, tongue-out moron, a puking mouth, or a winking eye. The winking eye indicates that whatever shit you just said was a joke, and the clever reader is in on it. I would gladly educate you with a chart of the various emojis available to you, if not for the fact I have not yet figured out how to insert the fuckers into this draft of Trailer Dogs.

Anyways, my point is, had Roseanne been smart enough to insert a winking-eye emoji after her contemptible tweets, we would have all known right away that she was "just kidding!" and that she was definitely *not* the half-witted, racist, Trump-worshipping moron she appeared to be. *(NOTE TO SELF: Ask old man how to insert winking eye emoji here.)*

And had Roseanne done that, we all might have forgiven her careless indiscretion, or written it off as an unfunny attempt at humor, akin to something Adam Sandler might be involved with. *(NOTE TO SELF: Ask old man how to insert crazy-eyed, tongue-out moron emoji here.)*

In conclusion, had Roseanne just used a little common sense and a well-placed emoji or two, she might still have the most highly-rated TV show in America. *(NOTE TO SELF: Ask old man how to insert frown, grimace, crazy-eyed, tongue-out moron, puking mouth, and winking eye emojis here.)*

There it is folks –The End of *Trailer Dogs* 3 *for sure this time!* *(NOTE TO SELF: Ask old man if there's a sorry, no refunds emoji to insert here.)*

TRAILER DOGS FAMILY ALBUM

Ben (Punkin' Head) the puppy

Punkin' Head & his toys (Note Ben's toy shirt, as described in TD1)

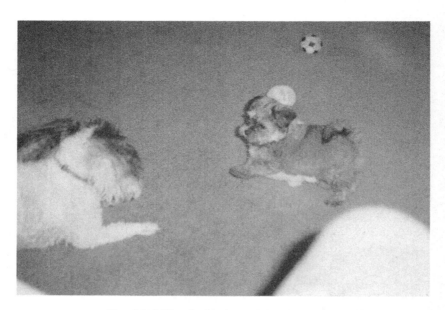

Punkin' Head playing with his sister, Holly

Punkin' Head studying computer programming

Ben & Cheekly the Rescue Chihuahua, snoozing during a road trip

Ben's lounge under the A/C
(We took the cushions off the sofa to make it easier for him to get up &
down)

Sully, watching TV in a motel room
(He especially enjoys Rachel Maddow)

Sully, napping on my old man

Sully & Boo, nap time

Me & my 3 sisters long ago
(Look closely. I think you'll spot which one is me.)

GLOSSARY OF BRITISH WORDS

Glossary	Where you are right now, looking up the meaning of British words
Cooker	What Brits call a stove, for christ's sake
Hob	What Brits call the burner on their stoves; (piss-pants maker)
Minge	What Brits call a woman's pubic hair
Loo	What Brits call their shitter
Mum	What Brits call their moms
Twat	What Brits call other peoples' moms
Sodder	What Brits call other peoples' dads
Beef curtains	What Brits call flabby or loose labia
Labia	What Brits call beef curtains if they are loose on a woman's hoo hoo (i.e., Melanie probably had surgery to repair her beef curtains.)
Rubbish	What Brits call Trump
Boot	What Brits call the trunk of their cars.
Bloody ass	What Brits call their boot when it's bloody
Holiday	What Brits call it when they go out of town and sit on their bloody asses for a week or two
£	What Brits call money

BEFORE YOU GO……

"Flight of the Trailer Dogs" is Book 3 in the Trailer Dogs Chronicles. If you haven't read the first two volumes, you've missed out on some really good shit!

Check out the first 10% for free by following these links to our gooood friends at Amazon:

Book 1

Trailer Dogs – Life in America's New Middle Class

Book 2

Revenge of the Trailer Dogs

If you'd like to contact me, my twitter handle is

@ellentrailerdog

and my website is

www.trailerdogs.net

(I'm not really the big asshole I pretend to be.) (Sort of.)

Thanks again!

Ellen

Made in the USA
Middletown, DE
31 July 2020